THE FAMILY CHUCKLE

Cover picture, *"The Home Place"* where we raised our family, is by Earl C. Brown of Selah, Washington.

THE FAMILY CHUCKLE

By Donna L. Scofield

A collection of columns, 2002 –2011

Copyright © 2011, Donna L. Scofield

ISBN 9781479282074

INTRODUCTION

A high school aptitude test showed I might be successful in two fields...plumbing or journalism. One year of college later I still couldn't decide which offered the best future for me, so I got married instead.

We were very lucky. Despite those surging late-adolescent hormones (we were only eighteen and twenty years old), the marriage stuck. I finished putting him through college. We moved to Yakima, in central Washington State, and raised four children while he taught school and I worked as a school secretary. During some of those years, a hearty chuckle was all that kept us going.

When the kids were grown and I had time to take a deep breath, I began writing a humor column called "The Family Chuckle" for our local newspaper, the *Yakima Herald Republic*. It was the perfect instrument of revenge. I could make the kids pay for all the gray hairs and heart palpitations they'd given me by embarrassing the socks off them, and there was nothing they could do about it.

It's been fun, and surprisingly enough, they're still speaking to me (most of the time).

This book includes most of those columns, in chronological order.

Donna L. Scofield

A special thank you to my friend Betty Van Ryder. She mentored me as a beginning writer, and provided valuable critiquing in all my work. Her efforts convinced the *Yakima Herald Republic* to sample my humor, resulting in a regular column. She's my combination agent/editor. Now if she only owned a publishing house!

October, 2002

BACK TO SCHOOL…HOORAY!

Have you moms recovered from back-to-school trauma? Maybe not. After all, the kids have only been in their classrooms for a few weeks. Give yourself time to heal.

It can be a multilevel crisis, ranging from a high level of ten (after-school day care) down to Level One (having the right pop star's picture on your kid's new binder). Of course these importance ratings are your own; your child might reverse them.

First there's the tension of classroom assignment. Some schools include the new assignment on the June report card, giving students all summer to consult older kids and determine whether or not the new teacher is an ogre who is going to make every waking moment a nightmare. (Of course the older kids are going to say Ms. Goodheart graduated from a coven, not a college. How cool would it be to say you had a lump in your throat when you told her goodbye on the last day of school?) At other schools, the list is posted in windows as the final duty on the Friday before Labor Day, giving the office staff a chance to make it to the parking lot before a complaint surfaces.

Then there's the matter of clothing. What mother wants to scar her child for life by dressing her in a Disney tee when the latest rap star is clearly what's in? The only way to be perfectly confident is to watch the Nickelodeon channel for the last three weeks of August, and shop for what those ten-year-old-going-on-thirty kids are wearing.

I recall putting the last stitches in a new pants outfit for a picky daughter at two a.m. on the first day of school, after being unable to find the right thing at the mall. (I keep a file of these self-sacrificial events. All of my children were ridiculously easy births, so I have no thirty-six-hour labors to use as guilt leverage.)

The just-before-school haircut is as important to the boys as the right outfit is to the girls. One summer I was inspired by a friend who taught herself to cut hair, so I bought the scary, pointy, sharp scissors, the special comb and most importantly, the electric clippers. I was sure I was going to save loads of money. My husband, a teacher, flatly refused my services. "Listen, the beginning of school is important to me, too," he said. "How would you like to introduce yourself to middle-school kids all day with a weird homemade haircut?" I was stung. "The haircuts aren't going to be weird," I argued. "Prove it," he responded briefly.

So I started on the younger son. I never got to the older son. He locked himself in his room after he saw his little brother. It was that darned "evening up" that did me in. I tried to blame it on the way he cringed whenever I came close to his ears with the chattering clippers, but it really wasn't his fault. After I had worked for a few minutes I stopped and looked at the back of his head. The hair was definitely trimmed much higher above one ear than the other. I carefully matched them up, but then the other ear was wrong. After the third "evening up" the child tentatively fingered the hair (or lack of) above his ear and shrieked, "What are you doing to me?" I was in too far to quit now. "Nothing," I said. "Not a thing. Relax; I'll fix it." Well, I fixed it, all right. The poor kid wore a baseball cap until Thanksgiving. School rules required removing it inside the classroom, but his teacher made a special exception in his case.

After clothes and haircuts, shopping for school supplies has to be high on the stress list. You have a general idea of what's needed, based on grade level, but since when has a mother's general idea been worth more than a scornful juvenile chuckle? You'd love to send Junior off on the first morning with just a pencil, Bic pen and package of notebook paper, because you know he's going to come home that afternoon with a complete list, based partly on what the teacher said and partly on what he saw come out of other kids' backpacks, but you don't want him to feel deprived, so you take him shopping for school supplies before the big day. It didn't take me long to decide that the thirty-six-hour labor I'd managed to avoid was pretty well equaled by spending an afternoon with a couple of sweaty kids in a store's school supply department, surrounded by other frazzled moms and sweaty kids, trying to decide what's hot and what's not in the field of binders and markers. Oh, and about Junior's list…if he says the markers have to be fruit-scented, or the word "Palm Pilot" comes up, be ready to call the school office for verification. As to the backpack…even though it'll be used for one hundred eighty days, it's not going up Mt. Everest on the back of a Sherpa, so don't stint on the weekly food budget for the top of the line model.

So just suck it up for a few more days, and it'll be over for another year. You can relax after next Tuesday. But don't relax too much. On the day I saw Matt, our older son (and at that time, youngest child) off to his first day of school, I drove away with a tear in my eye and a lump in my throat, already missing the part of my life that was finished. His little sister, Katy, was born the following June. Yeah. Count the months on your fingers.

October, 2002

AT HALLOWEEN, YOU ARE WHAT YOU WEAR

Okay, I confess. I'm a holiday junkie. I love Christmas most, but the other special days get me excited, too. Even Halloween. The bah humbug side of me mutters about giving kids license to beg, but my alter ego says, "Ooh, look at the cute little kitty," and tries to see anything at all positive about an adult holding out a pillowcase, ostensibly for the five-month-old baby in her arms, whose only costume consists of eyebrow-penciled cat whiskers, and who would probably end up in the emergency room if she ate any of the pillowcase's contents.

I love the costume part of the holiday. After my kids were too old for trick-or-treating as Raggedy Ann and Bobo the Clown, I put together outfits for their parties, and then the grandchildren came along and the fun began all over again. I've done all the old standbys, plus medieval princess, Hershey Kiss, Robin Hood, a giant bumblebee, and even a Tiny Tears doll costume for a fifteen-year-old. Oh, all right...there was that year I tried to talk them all into going as dice, which would have meant just cutting a head-hole in a cardboard box, painting it white, dabbing on black dots and hanging it from their shoulders. But that was a temporary aberration, a reaction to overwork. I came back full strength the following year.

Probably the best Halloween was the year granddaughter Caity was Little Red Riding Hood, wearing a hooded red cape and carrying a napkin-lined wicker basket for her treats. Her eighteen-month-old brother Steve was the Big Bad Wolf. I sewed his suit from long, shaggy artificial fur that wisped into my nose, balled up under the sewing machine needle, and is still, years later, showing up in weird places in my sewing room. Steve hated the costume. He bellowed his rage while we zipped him into it, shutting up only long enough to take a long, comforting drag on his bottle. Just as we were giving up and unzipping him, he caught his reflection in the darkened window and a big, wicked grin replaced the tears. Either the getup resembled something he'd seen in a cartoon, or there really is a little bit of the wicked wolf in every male. We had to forcibly remove his pelt at the end of the evening.

Undoubtedly the worst Halloween was the year it snowed. I was prepared for chilly weather, having learned to leave room under costumes for thick sweatshirts and sweatpants, but snow on Halloween? Whoever heard of such a thing? None of the kids could get into last winter's snow-boots. Our hobo's five o'clock shadow had been made by smearing his cheeks and chin with Vaseline, then dunking them into a thin layer of instant coffee spread on waxed paper (which sometimes has the beneficial side effect of turning the kid off the harmful effects of caffeine for life). The slush turned his whiskers into mushy espresso. The dripping skirt of Sleeping Beauty's gown trailed in the puddles and revealed itself as the bedroom curtain it originally was. Her blue eye shadow and rosy blush ran together, creating a face that the prince would not have kissed awake for all the gold in the kingdom. When the kids got home (early), the traditional homemade vegetable soup on the stove was much more popular than the candy in the treat bags, for the first time ever.

I haven't made costumes for awhile, but a holiday junkie never runs out of things to do. There's the haunted village to set up, pumpkins to carve, torches to light. If last year's balloon-and-cheesecloth ghosts are still presentable, we'll hang them in the birch tree. If not, there's still time to make new ones. Speaking of time…good grief! Where are the car keys? I still have to buy treats!

November, 2002

TRAVEL NOTES FROM THE EMPTY NEST

Returning from a spur-of-the-moment trip recently, we carried in our bags and settled down to catch up on the newspaper, and I had a flashback of trips with the four kids. There are some very positive things to be said for the empty nest.

Oh, those trips! In the same way that women forget the discomfort of pregnancy or they'd never have a second child, we always forgot the last vacation or we'd never go on another one.

First of all, there's no such thing as a spur-of-the moment trip with four kids. The event needs planning comparable to Hannibal's hike over the Alps. When the older two children were small, just packing the proper clothing was a major undertaking. By the time the younger two came along my standards had fallen. Changes of clothing for every possible situation were no longer required, as long as I carried a supply of cute bibs to cover the spit-up spinach stains left on the hand-me-downs by older siblings.

In addition to clothing, the variety of two trip necessities also changed over the years: in-car entertainment, and snacks.

In the beginning, for entertainment the kids enjoyed those wooden puzzles whose pieces made a nice thunk when bounced off the driver's head. Then they went through a sticker-book craze, when we learned that stickers glued on surfaces other than the book have a harmful effect on upholstery.

When they were able to read to themselves, we found that reading immediately brought on the younger daughter's carsickness. This also had a harmful effect on upholstery.

Next came the board games. We soon realized that manufacturers of travel games don't use magnets strong enough to keep the pieces in place when a poor loser whacks a gloating winner in the head with the board.

Family singing seemed like a *Parents' Magazine*, "Sound of Music" thing to do, so each trip included this activity. We sang exuberantly for twenty miles or so: "I'm a Little Teapot," "Home on the Range," and the first two bars of everybody's favorite camp songs, trailing off to a chorus of "Mm-m-m, yeah yeah, something something something."

The license plate game worked for only one trip, during which we realized that our older son shared the DNA for dishonesty with an uncle on his father's side. He alone sighted license plates from twenty-two different states during the first fifteen minutes of the game.

The carsickness-prone younger daughter was a source of entertainment for her sister and brothers. She made the trips under the influence of motion sickness drugs, which put her into a deep, but not deep enough, coma, from which she awoke periodically to snarl at her siblings and throw up. At the end of the trip the other three vied to see who could make up the most exciting account of sights she had missed, and get her to believe it. She might go for a famous rock group's tour bus, but she wasn't naïve enough to bite on Bigfoot.

Over the years snacks went from neat dry Cheerios in Tupperware containers to taco-flavored corn chips, which left a lingering aroma in the car that affected more people than just the carsick kid. Usually, by the time I pulled out my ace in the hole, the treat box, the kids were already bored and irritable.

Scientific experimentation taught our young learners that a juice box held at precisely the proper angle and squeezed with the right amount of force can shoot a purple stream into a brother's ear.

Once we had experienced our motorized version of the "Survivor" show and were home again, it was time to clean the debris from the car, track down the source of the horrible smell in the house (usually a carton of milk left on the kitchen counter) and do approximately twenty loads of laundry.

Now the nest is empty. With no pre-planning we can throw a few items in a suitcase and take off, never worrying about who got the window seats last time. We never have to say, "Don't make me stop this car and come back there!!" or answer that timeless question "When are we going to get there?" When we get home, it takes us a maximum of five minutes to empty the car, and neither of us has ever left a carton of milk out on the kitchen counter.

Like I said, the empty nest has some definite advantages!

November, 2002

THERE'S MORE THAN ONE TURKEY IN THIS KITCHEN

It's time to dig out that big roasting pan that's used twice a year, put all the leaves in the table, and get ready for Thanksgiving. When all the family is safely gathered in one room it may be crowded, but it's definitely a cause for giving thanks.

I can mess around with the menu for Christmas, but the dishes that surround the turkey at Thanksgiving dinner had better be exactly the same year after year, or I'll hear it from the daughter who thinks a tradition is anything you do the same way twice. I insisted upon varying things a few times, and they most certainly were not successes.

I decided it would be interesting and educational to have a dinner that was as close as possible to what the Pilgrims ate, and got a book from the library as a guide. I soon realized it wasn't going to be possible to be truly authentic. The kids said they absolutely would not eat Bambi, so the friend who offered venison had to receive a polite "no, thanks." They considered pemmican briefly, until learning it was made of dried fruit and animal fat. Stewed pumpkin drew a round of yucks. Indian pudding turned out to be sweet cornmeal mush, which they quickly decided did not deserve to be called a dessert. The boiled dried corn was like chewing slightly gummy BBs. But they did enjoy the authentic cranberries with our authentic turkey.

Even sticking to the good old traditional menu hasn't always guaranteed an uneventful Thanksgiving. The first time I hosted my husband's side of the family I forgot to take that little bag of innards they call giblets out of the turkey's cavity. If they'd stayed in there everything would have been fine, but I proudly carried the roasted bird to the table and after my husband carved it, all the relatives passed their plates and he piled on the meat and a big scoop of stuffing. Wouldn't you know my mother-in-law's plate would be the one whose stuffing included the mysterious little laminated bundle of internal organs? It became one of her favorite stories, told anew every Thanksgiving…one tradition I could happily have skipped.

Then there was the year when wigs and wiglets were all the rage. I felt so stylish until I stuck my head in the oven to baste the turkey and my cheap acrylic bangs melted.

The dinner I prepared right after I took microwave cooking lessons left me more exhausted that if I'd cooked it on an old wood range. I had to cut the turkey into quarters to fit it into the microwave. All those half turns and quarter turns, changes of power, "resting" times (the food, not me)…and I ended up with tough turkey, crunchy yams, grainy mashed potatoes and gravy that could only be described as strange.

A couple of years after that, I had the most relaxing Thanksgiving ever, and no messy kitchen to clean up. Luckily there were no guests that year, because we had dinner at one of those all-you-can-eat buffets. I put the turkey in very early, just to get it off my mind. It was still a little icy inside, so I set the timer to go on later and relaxed, knowing the bird would be roasted and the oven would be free later for the stuffing and the rest of the dinner. We read the paper and watched the Macy's parade, then some of us played Scrabble and the rest watched football. Eventually I wandered in to peel potatoes and suddenly realized something was missing. The air should have been rich with roasting turkey, and it wasn't. The timer hadn't clicked on. By this time we were starving, having just toast for breakfast in order to be hungry enough to really appreciate that turkey dinner, so we headed out to find food. Why the all-you-can-eat buffet, besides the appeal of heaped plates when you're famished? Maybe it was nostalgia. Years earlier, before our youngest child left toddlerhood and joined the civilized world, that was the only kind of restaurant we could visit. It was noisy enough to cover bellowing and table-kicking. We would wait until Shawn was really hungry, rush to the restaurant, fill our plates and eat fast, because when he was finished, the rest of us might as well be.

I can't wait to remind him of those good old days when we sit down to our civilized dinner…complete with non-Pilgrim foods, fully-cooked turkey, and an ambience slightly more genteel than what you find at an all-you-can-eat buffet.

December, 2002

TO DO – OR DIE TRYING

This time my holiday to-do list will really work, unlike those years that went something like this:

Dec. 1 - Start fruits and yeast for Friendship Fruit gifts. Fermented treat supposed to be wonderful on ice cream.

Dec. 2 - Make personalized Christmas cards from Martha Stewart magazine. Stir Friendship Fruit.

Dec. 3 - Buy more supplies for cards. Misspelled Christmas. Stir Friendship Fruit.

Dec. 4 - Write warm messages on Christmas cards.

Dec. 5 - Compile detailed gift shopping list. Accidentally use it to start fire in fireplace. Redo it. Look up wonderful crockpot recipe for tomorrow.

Dec. 6 - Head for mall with shopping list. Find four of sixteen items. Buy bunion pads. Canned soup for dinner because forgot to start crockpot.

Dec. 7 - Cut out four fleece jackets, eight pairs boxer shorts, six pairs flannel lounging pants. Stir Friendship Fruit every half-hour to make up for last three days.

Dec. 8 - Mix, freeze five different kinds cookie dough. Sew one fleece jacket.

Dec. 9 - Try mall again. Buy knee brace, orthopedic shoes for shopping. Find one more gift.

Dec. 10 - Rip out zipper from fleece jacket made day before yesterday. Re-sew. Throw in garbage. Sew two pairs boxers before realizing pattern cut on wrong size lines. No extra-small men in this family.

Dec. 11 - Bake two kinds cookies. Need decorative containers. Canvass neighborhood for empty oatmeal boxes. Make three into Nutcracker figures; run out of silver braid. Go to fabric store for more. Big sale on yardage. Leave in trunk to sneak into house when husband gone.

Dec. 12 - To mall again. Find one item on list, last one in store. Rip from hands of little old lady who thought she had it first. Will take cookies to nursing home in penance.

Dec. 13 - Finish shopping from specialty catalogs for kids. Stir Friendship Fruit many times. Skim off doubtful-looking gunk.

Dec. 14 - Bake more frozen cookie dough. Throw out batch burned while making Nutcrackers. Out of silver buttons for them. Go to fabric store. Sneak flannel for new boxers in house when husband is bowling.

Dec. 15 - Decide to make quilt for granddaughter out of scraps from everything ever sewed for her. Get out scrap boxes, start cutting.

Dec. 16, 17 – See Dec. 15.

Dec. 18 - Time getting short. Sew six pairs flannel lounging pants, finishing three a.m.

Dec. 19 - In bed with migraine until mid-afternoon. Bake last of frozen cookie dough.

Dec. 20 - Finish Christmas cards. Skip warm messages; have husband sign and address. Make three more Nutcrackers. Stop when two fingers painfully hot-glued together. Put rest of cookies on holiday paper plates. Try another fleece jacket. Stomp it; throw in garbage. Clean exploded Friendship Fruit from utility room ceiling; stir what's left.

Dec. 21 - Receive back-order notices for most of catalog orders. Write checks for kids. Make eight pairs boxers. Buying flannel twice means they now cost twice as much as retail. Search for gifts bought and hidden during year. Begin ornate wrapping. Frost, decorate some cookies with holly leaves and berries hand-sculpted from gumdrops.

Dec. 22 - Get back Christmas cards for no postage. Have husband write "Happy New Year" on envelopes, stamp, re-mail.

Elegantly wrap more gifts, then start stuffing things in used gift bags. Shop for decorative jars for Friendship Fruit. Make and freeze pies. Sew top of granddaughter's quilt.

Dec. 23 - Finish decorating cookies. No hand-sculpted holly; red and green sprinkles instead. Run out of holiday plates; put cookies in brown lunch bags. Send husband out to deliver. Do big grocery shopping at midnight. Lock keys in car; husband gets out of bed to bring spare. Grumpy.

Dec. 24 - Send husband shopping for gifts to accompany kids' checks. Can't face mall, goes to hardware store, returns with flashlight batteries, windshield scrapers, toilet plungers. Most fun he's had all month. Stuff some in used gift bags. Tie bows on plunger handles. Bulldoze gift-wrapping mess from spare room, tidy for company. Drain liquid from Friendship Fruit; throw shriveled, ugly fruit in garbage. Drink liquid. Coerce family into helping tie quilt. Run out of coordinating yarn; unravel an afghan and finish with crinkled purple and turquoise. Get to bed at five a.m. Christmas day.

Dec. 25 - Merry Christmas!

So why will this holiday be different? Because this year my list started on *November* 1!

December, 2002

SOLID GOLD MOMENTS

Past Christmases bring me chuckles, even though it took several years of distance for some of them to seem funny, such as the time the coal furnace backfired on Christmas Eve and the kids hung their stockings on doorknobs at Motel 6. (They loved it, and wondered why we couldn't stay in a motel every Christmas Eve.) Or the time a few days before Christmas when a teenage babysitter (who, needless to say, never sat for us again) found the closet where the gifts were hidden and showed the kids what Santa was going to bring them. Or the time my husband unwrapped only socks and underwear because I forgot to bring his golf cart down from the attic until December 26. Or the time my brother gave the boys supposedly tame (hah!) rats and they escaped into the house we were putting on the real estate market right after Christmas. Or the time I finished gift-wrapping at 5:30 AM, napped briefly, then watched the packages being opened at 7:30 AM.

But the Christmas I love to remember doesn't bring a chuckle. It brings the gentle smile that comes with looking back on moments that were solid gold.

Our older son, Matt, told me about solid gold moments. These are the times when you are completely happy, and lucky enough to realize it…not waiting for a promotion, or a raise, or for someone else to make your life complete. Matt had the ability to squeeze every drop of living out of life. His presence brought that joy to the rest of us.

I was usually too busy to recognize solid gold even if it bit me on the ankle, but there were a few times so precious that they stored themselves in that part of the brain that keeps every sensory detail of an event fresh and keen, as though it happened yesterday.

One of those solid gold moments came on a Christmas Eve. Our older daughter, Luanne, wanted her toddler, Caity, to experience the joy of falling asleep by the Christmas tree, as Luanne had as a child. Matt, home from California for the holidays, and our two teenagers, Katy and Shawn, decided to join them. Sleeping bags and pillows were hauled into the living room, the radio turned low to carols, and the only light was the glow from the tree. In the wee small hours of the morning I came into the room to turn off the tree lights. The air was scented with cinnamon from my baking, and the woodsy tang of the Christmas tree. I stood in the doorway and heard the wind sighing around the eaves of our old farmhouse, dying embers crackling in the fireplace, and the deep, peaceful breathing of my children and granddaughter. It brought me memories of making the rounds in deep night, tucking blankets around the shoulders of restless little sleepers. Gathered under one roof were the people most precious to me. I was blessed, and I knew it. It was definitely a solid gold moment.

By the next Christmas, Matt was gone. I thought there would never be another solid gold moment, but eventually they came again. Although there will always be a face missing in our circle, we honor the spirit of that son and brother with love and laughter. And I can bring out the memory of that solid gold moment, and warm my heart with its glow.

January, 2003

THE FAMILY HISTORIAN

The kids were all home for the weekend, and it's going to take a little while for the refrigerator to get back to normal. Right now it's in "full house mode."

I've read about guests peeking into their host's medicine cabinet out of nosiness, but I always felt a quick look in the refrigerator would give better information.

At the beginning, ours held bottles of formula and little half-filled jars of strained squash and pureed spinach; then it moved on to chocolate pudding, Popsicles and Kool-aid. The door displayed early primitive art…very early primitive.

About the time the kids began straggling into adolescence, the old fridge gave up the battle with one last, asthmatic wheeze. A motor transplant might have helped, but its problems went beyond mere motor. One shelf had been overloaded with gallon cartons of milk a few too many times, and just often enough to keep us on our toes, it would tilt and slide its contents out onto the floor.

Then there was that horrid fishy smell I could never remove. One Christmas Grandma slipped a seafood mousse into the defroster tray because there was no room on the shelves, and then forgot about it. As time went by and the mousse made its presence known, I sniffed through little foil packets of unidentifiable leftovers, never suspecting the defroster tray. By the time I found the mousse floating in a pool of ice water at defrosting time, it had dehydrated to the size of a Twinkie…a very pungent Twinkie.

The new refrigerator was a scientific marvel. All it lacked was a soundtrack to provide a musical background for the teenager standing with the door open, cooling off the kitchen while waiting for the leftover pot-roast to rearrange its molecules into pizza. It was self-defrosting. It also seemed to be self-emptying. For several years I could put $150 worth of groceries into it on Saturday, and by Wednesday all that remained was a withered lemon and a plastic bottle of chilled Coppertone. Soda vanished mysteriously through the cooling ducts. Salami folded itself into wafer-thin slices and slipped through the rubber gasket around the door.

The refrigerator door no longer displayed artwork. Instead it held a note pad on which teenagers were supposed to leave messages telling us where they had gone, so that when we got home from work to find the backdoor standing open and the furnace roaring in its attempt to heat the carport; the kitchen looking like Attila the Hun's mess hall; and stains that were either blood or catsup tracked into the living room, we would not be frightened. Sometimes the note pad held helpful messages: "Gone to town to price new glass for family room window," or "Call Roto-rooter," or "Don't open upstairs bathroom door – dog locked in," and written beneath that, "Watch where you step; dog sick." At other times there were messages of a more personal nature: "Mom, talk to me before you listen to anybody else – Matt," or, starkly, "I didn't do it – Shawn."

Now it's just the two of us, and the refrigerator door holds medical appointment cards and mundane reminders like "Take out garbage," and "Pick up dry cleaning." Inside you'll usually find yogurt and high-fiber snacks, with a good supply of Healthy Choice dinners in the freezer section. So for our own well-being I have to dump a bunch of soda, chip dip, cold-cuts and leftover desserts. No longer teenagers, the kids have lost the ability to empty a refrigerator in five days, and this "full house mode" has got to go.

January, 2003

GETTING CRAFTY

I'm thinking of starting a new club. At the meetings, we'll drink tea, eat cookies, and recycle each other's unfinished craft projects. I've got enough of my own to last through a year of meetings, at least.

Surely someone would enjoy the instruction book, three pairs of different size knitting needles, and four skeins of lovely coordinated shades of blue yarn. They were supposed to be made into an afghan, but during the fourth knitting lesson I decided that crafts are supposed to be *fun*, for heaven's sake. I was still one-and-a-half instructions behind the rest of the class, frantically trying to copy the person next to me so I wouldn't have to humiliate myself by raising my hand again. My pitiful work had been unraveled and re-knitted (or in my case, re-knotted) so many times that it had the texture of that crinkly Easter basket grass. So I dropped out. After all, afghans aren't that expensive.

Usually, though, my downfall is lack of time, not skill. Our youngest child is over thirty, but I've still got a partly finished Three Bears fabric house and a sampler embroidered with the first two letters of his name. I suppose I could rip out the "S-H" and redo it for a baby gift, but I've got to face facts. My friends are all past their child-bearing years, and besides, a pregnancy lasts nine months, and after thirty years my sampler is still incomplete.

And those pillowcases. I started to embroider a pair when I was recuperating from my hysterectomy. Unfortunately, I recuperated faster than I embroidered, so I now have one virgin pillowcase, and one with one-and-a-half purple pansies embroidered on it. By now I don't even *like* purple pansies.

Part of the problem is that in my original enthusiasm, I get carried away. The Christmas bells are a good example. I created a set of patchwork bells with jingly clappers to hang in a doorway, and they turned out so well that I decided to make some for relatives and friends. I got fourteen sets cut out, and a few of them stuffed with batting, and then it was time to get ready for Christmas, and then Christmas was over, and who wants to sew patchwork bells when it's not Christmas?

When the children were small I decided to make Winnie the Pooh stuffed toys, and learned there's a reason the Disney gift shop charges so much for those cuddly little creatures. I bought the Pooh storybook pattern, intending to make them all…Winnie, Tigger, Kanga, Roo, Piglet, Eeyore, and Rabbit. Winnie was the only one who made it out of the sewing room, limping badly due to one leg sewed in backwards. (Ripping out seams in terrycloth is enough to make a person keep Valium in the sewing machine drawer.) Whoever would have dreamed that little devil would consist of eighteen pieces of fuzzy golden terrycloth, all fitting intricately together to create his rounded tummy, honey-sniffing stubby nose and miscellaneous other body parts? I decided I wouldn't live long enough to make the whole ensemble.

The sack containing three pairs of off-white nylon anklets, Styrofoam balls, a tangled mass of brown yarn and fabric scraps dates from when I was going to make sock puppets for my grandson. I lost the pattern, but it really doesn't matter now, because he's getting his driver's license soon, so he probably wouldn't have time for sock puppets.

I know I'm not alone with my problem. I have a friend who started an embroidered tablecloth for her newly married daughter. Twenty years later she hung the part she had finished on a rod and presented it as a wall hanging…a very small wall hanging.

I think I'll invite her to my club.

February, 2003

SAVE ONLY THE BEST FOR POSTERITY

I had a wonderful idea for a Christmas gift this year for our granddaughter. Well, okay, so it was actually two years ago that I had the idea and started the cookbook. It turned out to be a little more involved than I thought, but it'll be an heirloom. No estimations, no pinches of this or that. There won't be any questioning phone calls when she prepares a dish for guests and it's a disaster because I forgot to list something important, like baking powder.

As I remembered some of my less than shining kitchen moments, I almost chickened out. There was the Mexican Chocolate Cake from which I accidentally omitted the sugar. It was chocolate hardtack, dense as a rock. I threw it out in the backyard and the dog, who usually loved leftover desserts, wouldn't even bury it. It was a cold, hungry winter, but the birds didn't peck at it. It spent the winter in a snow bank, and didn't become biodegradable until soaked by the spring thaw.

I remembered Shawn trying to tell me what he wanted for his fifth birthday dinner. "It's that meat that's black on top and has green stuff in it," he explained. It sounded dreadful and didn't ring a bell, but birthday dinner requests were always honored, so with a shudder I asked him what was usually served with it. When he told me it was "those potatoes from the oven with cheese on top," I realized he was describing scalloped potatoes, which usually accompanied my meatloaf. It had chopped green peppers in it, and ended up black on top because I usually forgot to cover it with foil toward the last.

And that blender breakfast. I hadn't stopped at the grocery store after work the previous evening, so that morning I had a choice of (a) serving a re-run of last night's dinner, which, truthfully, hadn't received good ratings for its premier showing, which explained the leftovers; or (b) making a tasty, high-energy blended breakfast drink of what was available: a box of frozen strawberries; the approximately two inches remaining in the bottom of the orange juice carton after the midnight marauder conscientiously did not drink the last drop; half a carton of wheat germ left from a prior attempt at Mother Earth cooking; three speckled bananas; four eggs, and unlimited dried milk. Unlimited because I bought the jumbo box, envisioning the kids drinking giant glasses of cheap, low-fat nutrition, but they turned up their noses at the taste and would only drink the stuff if I laced it with so much Hershey's chocolate syrup that the spoon stood erect in the glass. The children boarded the school bus that morning with a nourishing breakfast in their stomachs, but Matt, after questioning the contents of the blender, expressed gratitude that there hadn't been any leftover hotdogs in the refrigerator.

I determined this cookbook would be perfect. When I was long gone, it would be handed down from daughter to daughter over the generations. "Grandma Scofield was a little bit crazy, but she was a great cook," the older generation would tell the younger. My human foibles would be forgotten and I'd be this warm, fuzzy memory.

So I got out the manila envelope of recipes I'd clipped over the years, searching for the ones I had actually tried, not just clipped. I knew how long it had been since I'd sorted the contents when Nixon's resignation was featured on the other side of a newspaper recipe for zucchini pickles. I threw away recipes requiring more time in the kitchen than I plan to spend in this lifetime.

Next I began writing down actual measurements of ingredients in dishes I've made for years, which isn't as easy as it sounds. How much grated cheese is needed to make that old standby, macaroni and cheese, cheesy enough? When pot roast pan juices are thickened for gravy, do you pour off and measure the liquid before you thicken it? I did, for the cookbook. I don't want some future descendant calling her mother and asking, "Listen, was this Grandma Scofield person already senile when she wrote this thing, or did that come later?"

Caity was thrilled with the cookbook, so it was worth the trouble. After all, an heirloom can't be created without a little pain.

February, 2003

HEY, SOMEBODY PLEASE GIVE ME THE ANSWER KEY!

After years of motherhood I should be a fountain of knowledge, but instead I still have an ocean of questions:

As Infants:

- How can an infant who sucks three ounces from a bottle spit up a quart if you're wearing dry-clean-only and forgot to put a burp cloth on your shoulder?
- Why does a baby chortle and flirt with a weird man in an elevator, and shriek in terror when the grandma he hasn't seen for a month visits?
- Why does a child become sickest just after the pediatrician's office closes on Friday afternoon?
- How can a toddler who sneaks kibble from the dog's dish when your back is turned refuse yummy, fruit-flavored medicine out of a spoon?
- Why, at Christmas, do they ignore the expensive toys and play with the boxes they came in?
- Why does he become mute when you try to get him to say his newest word for a visitor, and babble it three times as soon as the door closes behind her?
- Why does the normally shy toddler tell the visiting minister exactly what Mommy yelled when she sewed her finger on the sewing machine?

After They've Left Babyhood:

- How can he outgrow expensive correctional shoes three times as fast as discount store sneakers?
- Why does she share with her class that Mama knows the vegetables are finished cooking when the smoke alarm goes off, but never something positive, like the fact that she cuts their cinnamon toast into animal shapes with a cookie cutter?
- How can they bring home safely all the fund-raising literature from school, but lose the notes asking for special parent/teacher conferences?
- When traveling, why do they never need to go to the bathroom when you point out the blue "Rest Stop Ahead" sign, but have an unbearable bladder attack when you're fifty miles from civilization?
- Why does she get carsick on the back of Mom's neck, instead of in the barf bag?
- How can he remind you daily that you haven't paid last week's allowance, but forget to tell you he volunteered you for three dozen decorated Valentine's Day cupcakes until 10:00 pm on February 13?
- How can they forget they have homework assignments when you ask about it after dinner, but remember them as they brush their teeth at bedtime?

When They Reach the Teenage Years:

- Why does she ask you which looks better on her, the blue top or the red one, and then wear the one you didn't pick?
- Why is it that when you offer advice it earns a scornful roll of the eyes, but when his friend says the same thing, it becomes a vital piece of information?
- How can the child who screamed and moaned with every DPTP inoculation now want her body pierced in so many places you're afraid she'll leak like a sieve when she drinks a glass of water?

- Why does the boy who had to be forced into the bathtub now take three showers a day?
- When a kid gets a driver's license, why does he jog for exercise but need the car for the trip to the corner grocery store?
- How can they leave perma-press clothing to wrinkle in the dryer because, although they were standing next to it, they didn't hear the obnoxious buzz when it went off, yet hear you uncap a soda from three rooms away and request a refill?

Finally, a Couple of Questions that have Plagued Me for Years:

- How can children who have been hell on wheels all day look so lovable and innocent when you tiptoe in to check on them as they sleep?
- And why was it that when my mother told me that one day I'd look back on those busy years as the best time of my life, I thought she'd lost her mind?

March, 2003

SOULMATES IN CHAOS

What are the odds, statistically, that descendants of a brother and sister who lived in New England more than two hundred fifty years ago would meet and marry, clear across the nation? Extremely slim. Yet that's the discovery my husband and I made.

After we bought our new computer and began exploring genealogy, we dug deeply into generations of topsoil, exploring our roots.

One morning when I sat down at the computer to search the internet for ancestors, I found a family tree for "Lamphere" on the printer, and filed it away with my papers. Soon my husband was searching for a tree he'd printed off the night before. I told him all I'd seen was Lamphere, one of my family names. "No," he protested, "Lamphere's mine."

We covered the kitchen table with print-outs and worked our way back to the early 1700s before finding our shared ancestors. His traveled west; mine trekked down to the Carolinas. "I knew we were soul-mates!" my husband exclaimed. "When I saw you that first day in college, I told my roommate you were the girl I was going to marry." I'd heard this story before. I'd credited it to the tight red sweater I wore, not that we were soul-mates. Now it looked like maybe he was right.

We decided to make a trip around the nation tracing our roots, and Westerly, Rhode Island, the site of our Lamphere connection, would be a highlight.

We started out in so organized and tidy a fashion. Who would have guessed it would turn to chaos? We packed lidless plastic totes for the backseat, so I could reach behind me and easily pluck out the item I wanted. One contained CDs. One contained magazines, road maps and AAA guides for the states on our route, arranged in the order we would use them. One contained healthy snacks. My laptop, with the power cord for plugging it into the cigarette lighter, was close at hand.

Before reaching Spokane we learned that the CD box slid forward and dumped itself on the floor at most stops. So much for my sorting by music type. We now listened to whatever my fingers closed upon. Clumsily re-folded road maps sprawled out of their tote. Sometime before Ohio, cracker packets split and their contents turned to sand in the bottom of the snack tote. By Connecticut, the bite-size Oreos and mixed nuts were all gone, but the dried fruit was just drier. Plastic bags of scenic brochures gave way periodically, carpeting the floor of the backseat.

Adding to the disorder was the fact that I was buying scenic postcards at every suitable location, and daily getting farther behind in writing notes on them. The plan was that each day I would update my travel journal on the laptop, write the cards and stop to mail them in the late afternoon. This worked fine in Wyoming, South Dakota, Nebraska and Kansas, but in scenic country, those tasks interfered with sightseeing. I began to wish we hadn't stopped in Pennsylvania to buy a new computer/cigarette lighter plug-in after I'd smashed the original one to smithereens in the car door. Soon I was spending my motel evenings trying to remember what exciting thing I could write on week-old postcards and what events to enter in the journal for last Tuesday.

Every morning we restored order (sort of), but by the time we were munching on our afternoon rice cakes, the backseat had once again taken on a life of its own. In historic areas, souvenirs joined the collection. By Kentucky, I no longer had any idea of what I had bought, whom I bought it for, and whom I had forgotten. I was just buying generic souvenirs and pitching them into the trunk, except for the books. Those I frantically tried to read before we got home to give them away as gifts, being very careful not to dog-ear the pages, or get crumbs in the binding.

It was a wonderful trip, although after driving for five weeks I figure it'll be quite awhile before either of us want to travel any farther than Seattle. But we'll always remember having dinner in an ocean-front restaurant in that resort town that was just a little farming village when my Theodosius Lamphere and my husband's Mary Lamphere folded their hands on the rough pine table, while their father gave thanks for food and family.

April, 2003

COCONUT CAKE AND SMASHED EGGS

Easter comes late this year, so it might be warm and sunny...a pleasant change from the ones I remember when the children were small. Most of those celebrations involved little girls with goose-bumpy legs, wearing sweatshirts over the frilly Sunday School dresses on which I had hemmed the last ruffle at about two that morning. Adults shivered while snapping pictures of one little cousin smacking another upside the head with his egg-gathering basket in a debate over who saw the purple egg first. Grandma borrowed a big down parka so she wouldn't freeze while she helped the child who was the least talented egg-searcher. "Under those daffodils! On that porch step! By the fencepost...no, not that one; the one right next to it!"

The kids had a list of requirements for what made a good holiday: lots of relatives, great food, candy, and presents. Halloween had only candy...but lots of it. Thanksgiving had just relatives and food; however, that extra day off school improved its popularity. Christmas, of course, was number one. Easter ranked right up there by Christmas. It had enough candy to keep them sky-high for a week. It had relatives who brought food with them, favorite dishes like deviled eggs, creamed asparagus, seven-layer salad and twice-baked potatoes, to go with the hostess's ham. And Grandma usually came through with presents. Like Christmas, Easter had it all.

The smell of vinegar and coconut brings back those Saturday nights before the big day. Vinegar was mixed with the dye in coffee cups on one end of the newspaper-covered kitchen table where the children colored eggs. Each child had the same number of eggs to dye, and of course one kid always rushed through and then tried to wheedle more eggs from the sibling who experimented with detailed wax drawings or time-consuming color combinations, and therefore had a tempting stock of pure white eggs left.

The scent of coconut drifted from the other end of the table, where I decorated the Easter cake with a nest made of green-tinted coconut, and filled it with jellybean eggs.

As the evening progressed cups of dye got spilled, and an egg or two always rolled off the table and landed with a repulsive splat on the floor. The dog licked up the coconut I dropped, but only nosed at the shattered eggs.

After the kids were in bed, we retrieved the empty baskets they had put out on the porch, and filled them with candy and little toys. At first we promptly put the filled baskets back on the porch for the kids to find in the morning, but the year the neighbor's dog found them first and ate all the candy changed that timeline. After that, one of us rushed the baskets to the porch when we heard the first stirring of a child.

Baskets were easy to fill when the children were small, but the older they got, the more expensive the baskets became. Chocolate eggs were still tempting, but one or two of the kids were dieting or guarding against zits, and gummy jellybeans played havoc with braces. Marshmallow Peeps and little fuzzy chicks were replaced by batteries for hand-held games, movie tickets, nail polish, lip gloss, and gas money. I was reluctant to let a childhood tradition slip from my grasp, but we finally decided a cute card with something green inside made more sense. The kids admired the presidential picture on the currency much more than they did the colorful bunny rabbit illustrations on the cards.

My sister-in-law hung on longer. She sent a big basket filled with candy, including the traditional huge chocolate, name-inscribed egg, to her son at boot camp. He called Easter afternoon to tell Ma he was a big boy now, and it was kind of embarrassing to receive a bunny basket. However, he confided just before hanging up, his buddies all told him to thank his mom for the candy. They really enjoyed it.

I've let the old tradition go. I miss shopping for little toys and filling baskets, and I miss the warm, Saturday night kitchen filled with the aroma of vinegar and coconut, but I have no trouble giving up the struggle to scrub dye stains off a table. And it's nice to know that come summer, someone else's dog will roll in that rotten egg that the kids didn't find!

April, 2003

TO GO, OR NOT TO GO?

I just got the notice about my high school reunion coming up this summer. I won't say how many years will be celebrated, because that would make too many people who currently feel ancient snicker and say, "Ah, I'm not so old, after all!"

The last reunion I attended was stressful enough, and I was younger, livelier, and better able to stretch the truth then. First came that form to fill in, to let your classmates know what you've been doing over the years. I thought long and hard. My boss said I was a great secretary and she didn't know what she'd do without me, so that must make me an ADMINISTRATIVE ASSISTANT.

Special interests…hmm. I bought a piece of Depression glass at a yard sale a while back…that means I COLLECT ANTIQUES.

I had a Tupperware party and gave a couple of baby showers; therefore I LOVE TO ENTERTAIN.

And I'm doing the office newsletter now, so I WRITE.

At the reunion dinner, those who hadn't returned the information form were asked to stand and catch us up. Duane, the party guy who barely graduated with a D average, surprised us all. He said he was an author, and we knew he was telling the truth because he wore a jacket with suede patches on the elbows and smoked a pipe. He told us we hadn't seen any of his books on the stands because he did scientific writing for the Johns Hopkins Research Center. He introduced his wife, a gorgeous creature with legs up to her shoulders and blond hair so long she had to flip it back when Duane seated her, so she wouldn't sit on her hair and snap her swan-like neck.

He was sorry his children wouldn't be at the picnic tomorrow; their daughter was at a Cape Cod retreat for creatively gifted children, and their son was at a summer camp for athletic Mensa students, to make brainy kids brawnier and brawny kids brainier.

As he spoke, my children were sulking at Grandma's house because they knew that at the picnic next day they were expected to make nice with people they didn't even know. I wondered if it was too late to rent a couple of kids who spoke three-syllable words and would smile adorably when they accepted the trophies for the day's athletic competitions.

Duane basked in his late-bloomer glory. Everybody mingled, glossing their tract houses into Tara and their numbly boring jobs into Indiana Jones.

When the event was ending Duane tapped on the side of the emcee's microphone to get our attention, and, probably having more fun than anyone else present, told us that he had met his "wife" when he picked her up at the escort service that evening; there were no children; and he worked at a plywood mill.

For me, the emotional high point of the event was when my husband met Ken, my tall, dark-haired high school boyfriend who had gone on to be an attorney. Ken was still tall, but it was hard to tell because, extremely drunk, he was crouched on a tabletop, doing that squat-and-kick-out Russian dance that can only be done well by native Ukrainians, which he is not.

His hair was still dark, what little was left. His beer-belly made a shirt button pop open during his dance. His mortified wife tried to talk him off the table, then snatched the car keys when they fell out of his pants pocket, and left without him. My husband, usually a kind and sensitive man, punctuated the drive back home by chuckling every fifty miles or so and murmuring, "So that was Ken. Hmm."

I don't know about this upcoming reunion. There might not be enough prep time. I'm not going unless I lose a quantity of weight that's possible only through surgery, have a good beautician cover Mother Nature's frost job with a better one, and get contacts. If there's an outdoor event requiring shorts, I'll need to get my varicose veins stripped. And, oh, yes…I'm not going unless I've published a novel by then.

So I guess my husband and I will just spend a quiet evening at home with the cat and some low-cal, high-fiber snacks. At least I won't have to worry about whether Ken has learned any new dances.

May, 2003

MOTHER'S DAY FROM HELL

This weekend we had our annual Spring Extravaganza, at which we celebrate four April, May and June birthdays and Mother's Day. It's like a mini-Christmas. When the last candle has been blown out and we're up to our ankles in crumpled gift-wrap paper, I like to ask the kids if they remember the Mother's Day from Hell, just to hear them groan. Then, since I'm basically a kind person, I change the subject.

On that fateful holiday our two older children, both on their own by then and both short of money, gave me wonderful homemade gifts in which time and thought replaced cash outlay. They didn't have a guilty role in the Mother's Day from Hell. But oh, those two younger children and their father. They didn't spend time, and very little money.

Our younger daughter, the Martha Stewart party-giver of her high school group, gave me a plastic pitcher to replace the one she'd taken to a party filled with lemonade, which had been taken home by someone else.

Our younger son gave me a one-quart Pyrex measuring cup to replace the one he'd broken when using it to pour water over the dog's head while giving it a bath in the family bathtub in my absence, thereby violating several rules at once. The most important rule he violated was that in order to prevent fur from clogging the drain, and just because of my own squeamishness, the dog is never to be bathed in the family bathtub.

A really great gift from my husband might have saved the day. And if anyone should have given a splendid gift to the mother of his children, it was Russ. He'd gone on a deep-sea fishing trip that weekend, dragging himself back home Mother's Day afternoon. I figured the trip must have been organized by a woman-hater. Why else would a bunch of husbands take to the sea on Mother's Day?

If he had given me a lovely, thoughtful gift, I might have felt sorry for the way miserable seasickness ruined his outing. This is the man who gets nauseated watching a movie about the ocean. When we rented "The Perfect Storm," he had to take to his bed with a cold cloth on his forehead and a barf basin by his side.

The only reason Russ was brave enough to sign up for the fishing trip was because a friend gave him a sample of a seasickness prevention device he was trying to sell. It was designed on the order of that patch behind the ear thing, said to work like a charm. It consisted of a piece of what looked like sandpaper taped to the stomach, scratchy side down. I would have thought it was a practical joke, except the patch-pusher was a straight-up kind of guy with absolutely no sense of humor.

When Russ staggered into the house, his first stop was at the bathroom medicine cabinet. He needed antiseptic and bandages for the large bleeding wound on his stomach where the patch had been. Later, when he was well enough to carry on a conversation, he said he'd decided the way the thing was supposed to work was to cause enough pain to take your mind off your seasickness. Every time Russ leaned over the rail to throw up, the patch rubbed his stomach. In spite of the pain, though, the seasickness persisted.

Although I felt sorry for this pale, sunken-eyed, bewhiskered, shabby man who looked like he had just stumbled out of a homeless shelter, his gift definitely did not save the day for his two children who were already deep in the doghouse. He gave me a handy little device to seal leftovers in plastic, which looked right at home with the plastic pitcher and big measuring cup.

I had prepared a festive Mother's Day dinner, and along with it I dished up huge portions of Guilt Ala Mode. Russ was able to sit at the table for a few minutes, until someone jostled a glass and the sight of the water lapping at the edge propelled him down the hall to the bathroom.

When he was well enough to drive, he took the kids to town and they came back with lovely, thoughtful gifts. I found a simple way to prevent a recurrence of the problem. In March I slap a list on the refrigerator door and secure it with a magnet. It's headed: "Things Mom Would Like for Mother's Day."

Works like a charm.

June, 2003

WHY SOME PEOPLE CRY AT WEDDINGS

Weddings may be beautiful, but there were a couple of them whose memories bring me shudders.

The first was our daughter's wedding. Counting on June sunshine, they planned a simple outdoor ceremony in a mountain meadow. Unexpected clouds threatened on the wedding morning, so the soon-to-be-married-couple, along with the father and brother of the bride, hung their wedding finery in the car, grabbed brooms and rags, and headed up Chinook Pass. The only roof on the site was a dusty, cobwebby ski shelter, which they would tidy up for possible emergency use. The bride's mother had the assignment of later leading the out-of-town guests in a motorcade up the mountain to the wedding.

I missed the exit off Highway 410, causing an eighteen-car turn-around. Once on the right road, we cavalcaded along until I had an uneasy feeling that we must have already passed the entrance to the meadow. When I dashed into the Goose River Tavern to ask directions, the patrons enjoyed my mother-of-the-bride dress...almost as much as they enjoyed telling me the Little American River turnoff was miles back down the road.

My sister-in-law took the wheel because it's not safe to drive while hysterical, and we headed back. At the turn-off I saw my husband standing by the road. His expression was not pleasant. "He'd better not say a word!" I sobbed. "Not a word!"

He said five words: "Have you got my pants?" When he'd grabbed the hanger, he assumed the pants were under the suit coat. They weren't. Soon a cousin of the bride came from the meadow's outdoor toilet shaking his head in confusion, wearing his uncle's dusty jeans and flannel shirt, followed by my husband wearing the young man's suit.

Eventually I was able to laugh about the day…sort of. But somewhere there's a family whose members probably get angry every time they remember their loved one's wedding. That's the other festive occasion I'd like to forget.

My mother-in-law, two sisters-in-law and I drove to Portland to attend a young nephew's baptism. We were late. I was driving and had trouble finding the church (it seems to be an ongoing problem). When we finally pulled into the parking lot on that hot Saturday afternoon, Grandma said she'd been there before and knew a shortcut. Tempers were short by this time, but I politely refrained from asking why she couldn't have directed me to the church, in that case.

We let her lead the way to the back entrance, climbing a short flight of outside stairs that ended in an open doorway at the top, from which music was drifting. As we entered the door strong organ chords introduced a familiar song, and I heard the sister-in-law behind me hiss "Wait! Wait!" But Grandma bustled on like a short, square little barge, and we trailed behind in her wake. We smelled flowers, and heard startled, but quiet, exclamations. My sister-in-law gasped, then muttered, "Oh, just keep going! Faster!" I kept my head down as we forged on, so I saw only the shiny black shoes of the father of the bride, and the filmy skirt of her gown as she pulled it aside when we met in the aisle. We three younger women cringed against the wall to let them pass while Grandma, head held high, steamed on.

In a brief, teeth-clenched conversation in the parking lot afterwards, Grandma said the whole thing would have been avoided if they'd had sense enough to keep that door at the top of the stairs closed, no matter how hot it was. And whoever heard of the bride coming up an outside aisle, anyhow? Anybody who got married in a church without a center aisle was just asking for something like that to happen! Grandma's daughter, who had an extremely strong sense of propriety, said just a few words: "We will never speak about this again! And Mother, the next time I say 'Wait!' you *wait!*"

When I remember arriving at my daughter's wedding late in a cloud of dust, leading half the guests, I tell myself it could have been worse. We could be the people still playing the wedding video, pushing "pause" at the entrance of four strange women, trying to decide which side of the family was responsible for inviting those rude people who came in the back door and met the bride coming down the aisle!

July, 2003

THE GREAT OUTDOORS

Ah, camping…the scent of sun-warmed pine; the sound of water gently lapping against river rocks lulling you to sleep; the sight of your family at twilight, singing around the campfire…what could be better?

Who am I kidding? I hated camping. If people were meant to go camping, we would have been born with the dents already in our backs, so we could match up with the rocks under our sleeping bag. If the Master Plan called for women to cook over campstoves, we wouldn't have been given eyebrows.

I married into a camping family. I think maybe my mother-in-law loved the outings about as much as I did. From the very beginning, she had stated that there would be no sleeping on the ground for her. A comfortable rollaway bed was brought from home and she slipped between clean sheets each night, while the rest of us hoped that the insect that had just crawled into our sleeping bag was non-poisonous.

We had a giant Scofield campout each summer. The super-organized sister-in-law must have had a friend who was a highly successful Tupperware party-giver, because she brought all her supplies in neat plastic containers. On one trip, as we washed dishes by firelight on the first evening, the other sister-in-law, the laid-back, carefree one, kept dumping more powdered detergent into the dishpan, trying to work up some suds. The organized one looked closely into the dishpan, then went to check her supply box. "You're never going to get suds," she said briskly. "You're using the powdered milk I brought for cocoa."

Because I had married into this camping family, and because everyone else in the world seemed to love the activity, I went along with camping to be a good sport. Besides, it was part of the parent's job description in those days. Back then, we even went camping when the mother looked at the sky on Saturday morning and knew in her bones that up at Mosquito Lake, it was going to start raining right after the tent was put up. By nightfall the rain was going to seep in the seams of the tent and drip on their heads as they balanced tin plates on their knees and ate beans and weenies the mother had cooked on the campstove in the rain. The ground cover would soak up the dampness like a wick and distribute it evenly under all the sleeping bags, which they would crawl into after an evening spent playing Hearts with a limp deck of cards by the light of the gas lantern, which hissed dangerously each time a drop fell on it.

Oh, those were the good old days. The kids remember them well, and so do I. They remember their favorite camp dinner, hobo stew. I remember the time the campstove gave a giant belch of flame that incinerated dinner and left me cowering in hysterics three campsites away.

They remember snuggling in their sleeping bags while Dad told the shiveringly scary story of "The Bloody Fingers." I remember the time Matt ate too many rich S'mores just before bedtime, got sick in the middle of the night and managed to throw up on four sleeping bags before I could get the tent door unzipped.

My husband and I talked it over, and I learned that at this stage of our lives, he's not much crazier about camping than I am. We're giving all the camping gear to our kids. They're young. Everyone knows suffering strengthens the character.

From now on, we'll do our camping at a nice motel, preferably one with a Jacuzzi in each room, and a good restaurant nearby. Beats cooking on a temperamental campstove, hands down.

August, 2003

OUR OWN WAIKIKI BEACH

We had an old standby vacation when the kids were growing up…the beach. Cheapness was the main advantage; my parents had a place at the beach. I always called it their beach house, but it was really a single-wide trailer. There is only one thing more depressing than vacationing in the rain at the beach, and that is to be vacationing in the rain at the beach with four kids in a single-wide trailer. Sometimes when we were all tucked into our bunks and daybeds, I would lie awake and wonder if there was enough oxygen in that tiny space to sustain us through the night.

Mom either loved to cook and care for all of us, or else she put up a good front. But when the folks weren't there, I wasn't thrilled about cooking and cleaning…heck, this was supposed to be *my* vacation, too. And just opening the refrigerator was a real test of courage for me. On one of our early trips we unlocked the trailer door and reeled from the stench. My brother had put a baggie of fresh clams in the freezer compartment during a visit, and the refrigerator died several weeks before we arrived. Scrubbing and airing never quite removed the aroma.

Even without cooking, a vacation at the beach was a lot like everyday life at home…only in a smaller area with fewer conveniences. And there was still the sand to be swept up several times a day.

My husband hated the beach. He hated getting sand in his shoes, and the long, unstructured days. Sometimes he would craftily bargain his way out of the trip, agreeing to do some monumental chore for the privilege of staying home.

When the weather was nice we loaded up our blankets, beach towels, sand toys, magazines, lunch, flip-flops, radio, and cooler full of sodas, and hiked over the dunes to the water. The day was not quite peace and relaxation for me. One of the children was so foolhardy that he would begin wading, then swimming, and be well on his way to Japan before I could wave him back in with a beach towel. One stayed up at the high-tide mark and spent most of the day reassuring herself that she was indeed going to go in the water very soon…just as soon as she was ready. It was still a little too cold. The other two kids ranged in between these two extremes. I would keep track of the four of them all day, and when we trooped back to the trailer in the late afternoon, I would spray sunburn pain relief on their shoulders. Except for the one who was afraid of the water. She never removed her sweatshirt.

As they grew up, the one who was afraid of the water lost her fear of it, and joined her brother in his quest for Japan, along with the other two. For awhile I thought about getting a Labrador Retriever as a lifesaving backup, but cramming a wet dog into that vanload of kids and junk might have caused me to walk into the ocean without a backward glance.

We all see a different scene when we look back on those trips. I remember the sun-filled days by the water, but a vision of the trailer's steamed-up, rain-streaked windows lurks there somewhere. The kids say they remember best the summer I made them all fill their sand pails with wild blackberries that grew in the lane, so I could make jelly when we got home, but I think they're just trying to lay a guilt trip on me. My husband remembers the year he got to stay home by painting the kitchen and bathroom. That guilt trip's not going to stick either. I just remind him that my folks' friends at the beach thought their oldest daughter was a brave single mother, bringing her kids on a cheap vacation.

He loves the beach now. Since it's just the two of us, we can stay at an ocean-front motel. The closest he gets to the ocean is the promenade. You never get sand in your shoes there.

September, 2003

OVER THE PRAIRIE AND THROUGH THE PLAINS, TO GRANDMOTHER'S HOUSE WE GO

We enjoyed our trip to the Midwest this summer. We made frequent break-the-monotony stops for lemonade or postcards, or to check out local tourist attractions. As we drove through Iowa in our comfortable, air-conditioned rental car, beautiful music coming from the CD player, I had a horrible flashback of the trips to Missouri to visit grandparents when I was a child.

Those treks were exercises in human survival. They were always in midsummer, and the car wasn't air-conditioned. With all the windows down, hair tangled and lips cracking in the hot wind, we zoomed across the miles of flat prairie. The open windows didn't keep us any cooler. The only benefit they offered was that the rush of wind kept my parents from hearing the noise in the backseat, unless the fighting went beyond sibling rivalry to out-and-out fratricide.

I'm much older than my sister and brother, so I was made the caretaker of the backseat. I sat in the middle, with the assigned task of keeping them from fighting. I gave up on that effort well before reaching Boise, and immersed myself in a book while they reached behind, around and over me to pinch and pull hair. When the battle got so violent it interrupted my reading and I tried to restore order, that job was further frustrated by my little brother's belief that if he couldn't see us, we couldn't see him. It's hard to successfully intimidate a smirking little boy with his eyes squinched shut. I wanted to slap him into the middle of next week, but that wasn't allowed.

About the time I became a self-centered teenager, I realized that the pink felt skirt with the appliquéd poodle, and the matching cashmere sweater that I'd been wistfully yearning for, wouldn't even make a dent in the amount Dad was plunking down at gas stations. From then on, my surly uncooperativeness added another layer of tension to the stifling atmosphere in the car.

Dad kept a record of how long each trip took, down to the minute, with the goal of shaving time off the previous record. This meant that you'd better go to the bathroom when he stopped for gas, because the car wouldn't stop again until the tank was empty. Midway during the trip he'd have to get the oil changed and a lube job, and Mom took advantage of that to run to a nearby diner and order burgers to go. The rest of the meals were mostly baloney slapped between two slices of bread and handed back to us by my mother.

Mom didn't drive, so there was nobody to share the load, but that didn't change Dad's goal of driving straight through without stopping at a motel. My mother's terrified shriek when he almost drove into the back of a semi, or some other sleep-deprived near-disaster, always put a stop to that dream. If we were near a town we'd check in and spend a few hours in a cheap motel. If we were in the middle of nowhere, we'd sleep in the car until Dad was ready to drive again.

Somewhere in Wyoming, Mom and Dad began the discussion about which side of the family we were going to stay with first, and for how many days. They could have lasted the whole trip without reaching agreement, but after several hundred miles they dropped it, both evidently (and mistakenly) thinking that the other would soften before our arrival.

The problem was solved by Dad's migraine, the result of driving two thousand miles with very little sleep. The hours he had gained over the last trip were spent lying in a darkened room with a cold cloth over his eyes. We went to his family first, knowing that the houseful of people at Mom's home wouldn't tiptoe and whisper for however long it took the headache to abate. She was the oldest of nine children, and when the whole extended family gathered, the noise level approached riot.

By now I would have stayed at Jack the Ripper's house if it meant getting out of that backseat wind tunnel, and I would have cheerfully sold my little brother and sister to the highest bidder. Luckily, the horrors of the trip faded during the next two weeks of being pampered and catered to by seldom-seen grandparents, aunts, and uncles. If the memory hadn't softened a bit, there was no way we could have piled into that car for the two thousand mile drive home.

Is it any wonder that our drive through Iowa this summer seemed like a trip through Paradise?

September, 2003

THE ULTIMATE MULTI-TASKER

Now that the kids are back in school, it might be kind to take a moment to appreciate the person who has carried multi-tasking to a whole new level: the elementary school secretary. This is the woman who directs a child to the box of donated clothing for dry underpants after an embarrassing accident; answers the phone; works on a computer budget program; and wipes vomit off her own shoe…all at the same time. And she knows that when she leans close to the next head-scratching kid to apply the fine-toothed comb and magnifying glass, she'll hear high-pitched little lice voices piping, "Let's pa-a-a-rty!"

When I first started working as a school secretary, I thought it would be like any other job. Little did I know that along with clerical skills, a good school secretary needs the sweetness of Mother Teresa, the wisdom of Solomon, the eyes-in-the-back-of-the-head ESP of motherhood, and one other ingredient…a slight degree of craziness, to cope with the things kids do and say.

One thing that spices up the job is a child's tendency to utter off-the-wall comments without fear of embarrassment. One Monday when I showed up with a new hair-do, a little girl leaned over the counter and tugged gently at a curly lock. "See, I told you it wasn't a wig," she calmly told her friend, and they walked away.

A principal I worked with took a stopwatch out at recess to time impromptu races, which the kids loved. Unfortunately, he had a long name. On a day when other duties kept the principal in his office, a first-grade boy approached my desk. "Could Mr. Cher…Mr. Cher…could your daddy come out and play?" he asked plaintively. "Cherrington" was just too much name for the boy's tongue to get itself around.

Another child managed a big word a bit TOO successfully. His mother reported to me that when she asked her son how school had been that day, he replied, "Pretty good, even if we did have a prostitute." Stunned, she asked for details, and Jeremy said, "Yeah, Miss Brown was sick, so we had a prostitute." When I relayed the conversation to the substitute teacher, she wondered if she should get a leather mini-skirt and stiletto heels to wear next day.

Meeting kids outside the school setting can be interesting. A youngster whose attention deficit disorder required me to carefully dole out and record his Ritalin medication each noon spied me when I was shopping. "Hi, Mrs. Scofield!" he yelled enthusiastically across several Bon Marche aisles. "Hey, Mom, there's the lady who gives me drugs!"

Most of the "wisdom of Solomon" part of the job takes place in the health room. Is this child sick, or just sick of math? The good old thermometer is the tried and true test. As I popped one under a fourth-grader's tongue for the third morning in a row, I was pretty sure he would soon be heading back to class. He did have a fever, though. He would have gotten home free had he not overdone it a bit. As I took the thermometer from his mouth he said, "See, I told you I was really sick this time!"

I saw the mercury level and gave Jason my best steely-eyed mother look. "Okay, there's no way you've got a temperature of 106°. How'd you do that?" I demanded. Jason was even less successful as a liar than as a mathematician, and crumbled instantly. He was doing well in science, though. By rubbing the thermometer vigorously with his flannel shirttail, he had proven the theory about friction producing heat.

I could never understand why sometimes the child who finds a secret way into your heart is the opposite of the sweet, tractable, obedient kid a sensible person would prefer. Karen, the other secretary, and I dealt daily with a little red-haired firecracker...doling out his meds, cleaning and bandaging the scrapes when the Ritalin didn't prevent fighting, calming him when he was a hairsbreadth away from losing it and getting suspended again. When his morning dosage was eliminated, we even bought a supply of cheap little toys, and he earned one each day he stayed out of trouble until the lunchtime pill.

Then he moved. When he came to tell us goodbye, he impulsively threw his arms around the other secretary's waist, and said sadly, "I'm going to miss you, Mrs. Herndon." Then he did the same with me. As we watched him leave, Karen said, "Well, there goes trouble with a capitol T!" I agreed with her. She grabbed a Kleenex off the desk and said, "Then how come we're standing here with tears in our eyes like a couple of idiots?"

Neither of us knew the answer. It had to be that slight degree of craziness.

October, 2003

BOARD GAMES FOR THE BORED

I cleaned the den closet the other day, and gazed in dismay at the huge stack of puzzles and games that saw frequent use when the kids were all home. Now they're brought out only at Christmas, and some not even that often.

We started with cribbage when we were first married and couldn't afford a TV. Then there was the canasta rage in college, when us young-marrieds with no entertainment budget took turns providing a flat surface for the cards and a variety of flat surfaces for the bring-along babies to sleep on, because hiring baby-sitters was definitely out of the question. We served coffee and whatever snack was cheap and filling.

My husband grew up in a family that loved cards, so when we spent time with his brother and wife, pinochle was the after-dinner thing to do. However, the men took their cards seriously, while my sister-in-law and I talked. At some point in the evening my brother-in-law would slap his cards down on the table and demand, "Are we playing cards or yakking? Take your pick! One or the other!"

I'll have to admit that chatting caused us women to lose focus, so to level the playing field we resorted to cheating. We let each other know what suit we wanted by casually pointing to an engagement ring for diamonds, discreetly patting the chest for hearts, mentioning social groups for clubs, and gabbing about digging in the garden for spades. But sometimes we were having so much fun talking that we didn't even catch each other's signals. However, the men were paying strict attention to the game, so it didn't take them long to figure out what we were doing.

When the kids got old enough to play games, there was Candyland, Uncle Wiggly, Chutes and Ladders, and Old Maid. Being too busy was a better excuse than boredom for not playing with them, but even when you've got enough work piled up to keep you busy until menopause, you can't turn down a sick child who wants to play Old Maid. The result was afternoons that seemed thirty-six hours long.

They eventually graduated to Monopoly, which turned children into bloodthirsty land barons who made Leona Helmsley seem generous by comparison. They thought nothing of throwing the woman who had given them life and breath out into the snow, homeless. I did some serious rearrangement about which kid was going to get my antique Carnival glass collection when I was gone. The recipient changed with each game, until I finally decided none of them deserved it. They put a hotel on every slum property they got their greedy little fingers on, and cackled gleefully as the unlucky tourist landed on it. When a sibling drew a card saying "Go straight to jail. Do not pass Go. Do not collect $200," they displayed the kind of joy usually caused by the words, "The double-chocolate-chip cookies are cool now, and you can have as many as you want."

Then we moved into the era when the kids' brains had reached adult capacity, and the adults' brains seemed to be slipping back toward Candyland level. We now made all kinds of interesting discoveries about personalities and abilities. We learned that the two daughters excelled in word games, as I did, and soon we could only play Scrabble with each other. The males of the family refused to take us on. We learned that Shawn could draw a picture in just a few seconds that would make his partner instantly guess the Pictionary word. We learned that Matt mastered any bluffing game by looking into your eyes with an intense, honest gaze and swearing that some piece of nonsense was absolutely true. He also was not above smacking a jigsaw puzzle piece into place with his fist when he had tried it in the same location five or six times. We learned that a ticking timer freezes my brain into inactivity until the moment the timer dings, when I blurt out the answer I should have given earlier. We learned that those counseling-type games where you predict how your partner would act in a situation are best played with friends, not family. They can sulk and yell at their own house, and be in a good mood by the next time you see them.

After all that nostalgia, and because I was getting tired, anyhow, I left the games and puzzles in the closet. Winter boredom will soon be here. We'll give them one more try.

October, 2003

AH...HALLOWEEN BEFORE RAZOR BLADES IN APPLES

I thought I'd never reach this stage, but I've got to borrow a phrase from the *Old Fogy Handbook*. We're always hearing "They just don't make (fill in the blank) like they used to." Well, they just don't make Halloween like they used to.

I was at Costco buying Halloween treats when I made this realization. This was my second expedition. When I shopped a few weeks ago I made the mistake of getting mixed candy bars. Then my husband read that research has determined chocolate is good for the heart and blood pressure, and there went the Hershey mini-bars. A friend gave me the recipe for Snickers salad, where tart apples, pecans and chopped Snickers bars mingle in a bed of Cool-Whip and turn into ambrosia. There went the Snickers mini-bars. It was so delicious I tried it with Milky Way bars, but that was a waste of perfectly good candy. So I was back at Costco, looking for something good enough to keep the trick out of trick-or-treat, but at the same time not good enough to get eaten before the holiday.

Those King Kong-size bags look large enough to stock a small candy store, but I've learned that one bag is never enough. I always say I'm going to hand out only one treat per kid, but if the child is one I know, or has an especially cute costume, or dimples, or says "Twick or tweat" with a sweet little lisp, I can't stick to my rule. They get more. I can stick to the rule only when the kid on the doorstep is taller than I am.

I should turn the door duties over to my husband, but he says things that make me want to run out and check our car for slashed tires...things like "Are you from around here, or did you come in on the Greyhound?" or "You're kind of old for this, aren't you? Which high school do you go to?" I, on the other hand, avoid eye contact, drop a piece of bubblegum into a pillowcase and hope they don't egg the house.

At Costco, I looked at that candy stretching off into the distance and remembered my childhood Halloweens.

We lived in the country, which meant that we really earned that treat with our long walk between houses. To make the walk distasteful, there was Mother Nature's rule that in the Portland/Vancouver area, there must always be rain on Halloween…enough rain that when you stepped in puddles in the dark, the water came in over the tops of your galoshes. Enough rain that unless the popcorn balls or homemade cookies were securely wrapped in waxed paper, they were mush by the time you finally got home. Ah, yes, these were the good old days before razor blades in apples. In addition to popcorn balls and cookies, we could look forward to homemade fudge and penuche. One neighbor always gave us her special banana nut bread, but that was a little too wholesome to be appreciated, and usually ended up in Dad's lunch bucket the next day.

The only bad memory of those Halloweens took place at a house that stayed undisturbed after the first year we stopped there. The residents were a very elderly brother and sister, and they had us all come in and sit down for prayers, hymns and a short sermon. When the service ended, they gave us each a wormy apple. Back outside in the rain, we all threw our apples against the front door and ran.

The best memory was provided by the minister of the little community church. His wife invited us into their warm kitchen, which was filled with a lovely smell of baking. While the minister hung our wet coats over the furnace register, and upended our galoshes on it to dry a bit, his wife seated us at their kitchen table and served us waffles hot off the griddle. When we had eaten all we wanted, she poured us hot chocolate and set marshmallows afloat on the rich, dark liquid. I was so impressed that I wanted to drop out of the church our family attended, and join the First Church of Waffles, but my parents wouldn't let me.

Well, as the old saying goes, that was then and this is now. I wonder how many kids would run screaming into the night if I invited them in for waffles and hot chocolate?

November, 2003

ADVENTURES IN THE PRODUCE AISLE

I've decided there's one activity that should be a one-woman, Lone Rangerette project, maybe even more private than shaving your legs or tweezing those pesky little chin-whiskers. That activity is supermarket shopping.

Children are a definite shopping handicap. As soon as they are able to sit up safely in the kiddy seat, they decide they want to ride inside the cart itself, so they can mutilate merchandise without having to reach so far to get to it. Also, if they're riding inside the cart, they're a little farther from your eyes, so you're less likely to notice them when your attention strays and they sneak something off the shelf and into the basket. These forbidden items are the ones they immediately vandalize, knowing mother is too honest to put damaged stuff back on the shelf. The kids are especially active in the cereal aisle, stowing away boxes of Candy-Coated Madness Flakes or Sweety Oatums, with a sugar content so high that when you add milk to the cereal bowl and the sugar dissolves, you're left with about two tablespoons of nature's own grain.

When they're not concealing a box of Sweety Oatums under the family-size package of toilet paper, they're throwing noisy hissy-fits for items you refuse to buy. I'm sure you've noticed little racks of toys scattered throughout the store…the kind designed to self-destruct by the time you get to the parking lot. That's called creative merchandising. Just when you think you can safely concentrate on choosing the detergent that does the least damage to the environment, hanging there in front of the fabric softeners is one more thing your child absolutely cannot live without. Then you have three choices: (1) leave a cart full of groceries in the aisle and go home; (2) through clenched teeth, hiss threats of a time-out that will last through puberty; or (3) buy the piece of junk.

When the children become teenagers, they would rather die than go to the grocery store with their mother, unless it means they get to drive the car, or they've just turned vegetarian and figure Mom isn't smart enough to find the Boca Garden Burgers and tofu. Except for these rare occasions, there follows a time of serene, solitary supermarket shopping. Then your better half retires, and is sometimes so bored he goes along for the ride. Except he calls it "helping."

Helping? This is the man who won first prize in the "Dumb Things Husbands Do" contest we wives held at the office. He called me at work from the grocery store because he couldn't find a package of one dozen tortillas, which my list specified. He complained that none of the packages listed how many tortillas it contained. Further questioning disclosed that he was looking at packages of tortilla *chips*, not tortillas.

There's irony in this "helping." I agonize over labels, trying to decide which is worse, two zillion mgs of sodium or fifteen grams of fat, for the benefit of the man who is bumbling through the baking section. He's looking for the Boston cream pie mix that went off the market at least twenty years ago, but no big deal. It wasn't as good as the one his mother used to make anyhow. And hey, it wouldn't be too hard to make from scratch, would it?

While I'm deciding which fresh vegetable would nutritionally complete the meal and at the same time provide esthetically pleasing color contrast (the only concept I remember from home ec class), he is resting his forearms on the cart handle, staring into space and wondering if he'll be home by the time the ballgame starts. Occasionally, if it's the dead of winter and you'd have to sell an organ to pay for them, he'll rouse enough to say something helpful, like "Asparagus would be nice," or "We haven't had fresh raspberries for awhile." When I've had all the help I can handle, I send him in search of some elusive item on the far side of the store. Sometimes, just for the sheer evil fun of it, I make up an item that doesn't exist.

I guess things could be worse. So far we haven't had any public hissy-fits. He hasn't had to have a time-out. However, I'm going to have to start examining the cart contents before we get to the checkout stand. I don't want to embarrass him by sending him to put items back on the shelf, but those smoked oysters he hid under the toilet paper last time were darned expensive.

November, 2003

BLESS THEM ALL

A few years ago I stood in the grocery store line after work, doing my Thanksgiving dinner marketing, definitely not in the best frame of mind. I was tired. My feet hurt. I'd left a half-solved problem at the office, which I knew would be waiting for me when I returned. My hair was straggling down my neck, and I didn't have time for a perm before the holiday. I couldn't even wear my wiglet because a few years back, I'd stuck my head in the oven to check the turkey, and melted the bangs (needless to say, this was a cheapie, acrylic item). I'd forgotten my list and was winging it, so I'd had to get out of line and go back for forgotten items three times. My cart was heaped and overflowing, which meant the checking account was going to take a real hit.

I knew I should be glad my whole family, and my parents, would be gathered around our table for the holiday dinner, and I *was* grateful. But I also felt stressed and over-burdened.

Then I became aware of the people around me, and my problems took a backseat. I saw an old, old man buy a turkey TV dinner and a frozen pumpkin pie. Reading between the lines, it was obvious that he was spending the holiday alone. I heard the quiet conversation going on between the young couple behind me, as they pulled out of line. "Let's take that turkey back and get a stewing hen," the woman said. "Both kids need new shoes; it's too cold for sneakers. And we don't have to have fresh cauliflower. Canned green beans are much cheaper."

In the next aisle, a couple was arguing in a way that suggested the trouble was ongoing, and probably wasn't going to take time off for the holiday. "What do you care? While your mother tells me how I *should* have made the stuffing, you're just going to be watching football!" the wife flung over her shoulder as the husband slouched off to the magazine rack.

I realized how much I had to be thankful for, and wrote the check without even gasping at the amount. We had our big, festive dinner. All the kids were home. Mom and Dad came up. I cooked like a fiend, and we had to bring in the kitchen utility cart to hold the extra bowls and platters. We ate ourselves into oblivion, then played board games, watching football on TV when the crowd's roar made us think we were missing something extraordinary. In the evening we finally got around to the pies, followed by cold turkey sandwiches and Alka Seltzer around midnight.

My folks were with us again the following Thanksgiving, but this time when Dad said grace, he added a new phrase:" Bless the one no longer with us." Our older son was gone. Drifting in and out of awareness just before he died, Matt had described what he was picturing in his mind. "I just saw the neatest thing, Mom," he whispered. "I saw us all at the table at Thanksgiving, eating that good turkey dinner you always fix, and then I saw us around the Christmas tree, opening gifts."

As autumn neared the first year after Matt's death, those words played over and over in my mind. Although hearing them brought such pain, I would never wish them unsaid, because it comforted me to know our son died remembering the warmth of home. Still, I had to force myself to cook that first turkey dinner and trim that first Christmas tree without him. Life goes on for everyone who's left, so I did what was required, but I realized the truth of what our younger daughter had sobbed after her brother's death: "We'll never be a whole family again. There'll always be part of us missing."

In a couple of years, Dad was no longer there to give the blessing. A few more years, and Mom was gone.

The rest of us still have the big dinner. I stuff the turkey, and bake the pies, and we play board games and watch football. We enjoy the day, and each other. Whoever gives the blessing says, "Bless those who can't be with us."

Time has distanced the pain…not removed it, just taken it farther away. Now, in my heart I can add, "and thank You for the years we had with them." There are some blessings too great to ever take for granted. The ones we love may die, but they are never really gone. A part of them stays with us forever.

December, 2003

CHRISTMAS BY TIME TRAVEL

I've been traveling into the past by time machine for the past week. My time-travel vehicle is a stack of old *Good Housekeeping* magazines I found at my aunt's house in Portland. They go back so far that they include the childhood years of all four of our children. My husband paled at the sight of all that paper, but we reached a compromise. He said he'd find room in the car for just the November and December issues if I stopped pestering him to haul home the whole stash.

Once home, I sorted them chronologically, got comfortable, and began my trip into the past through the holiday issues of the magazine that defined the kind of mother I wanted to be at that time.

Every December I happily replicated the homemade decorative treat that graced the cover of each issue (all proudly proclaiming "Our Best Christmas Ever!") One year it was a gingerbread house; another time a huge Santa cookie perched atop a one-pound coffee can transformed into a drum with frosting and candy trim. No matter how challenging, it was my goal to turn every Christmas into a *Good Housekeeping* holiday, right up until I went back to work and realized there weren't enough hours in the day to make a village out of cookie-covered milk cartons.

When I stopped chuckling at the ads of housewives waxing the kitchen floor in high-heels and pearls, while they joyfully exclaimed over the lack of waxy yellow build-up on the linoleum, I settled down to the important stuff…remembering those Christmases.

I remember feeling badly that we couldn't afford a new Christmas outfit for two-year-old Luanne; and how cute she looked when I appliquéd a big candy cane to the front of a red pinafore she hadn't quite outgrown.

I remember Russ and I putting together a three-piece child-size kitchen made of heavy cardboard after the kids had gone to bed Christmas Eve. We began easily putting tab A into slot A, and then it got complicated. Around two a.m., when we realized we had the oven door on the front of the sink, we frantically re-read the instruction sheet and learned that even toy manufacturers can have a sense of humor. The last sentence on the sheet was, "Do not attempt this process on Christmas Eve."

I remember happy weariness as I stuffed stockings in the wee hours of Christmas morning.

I remember the hectic joy of having Russ' entire family for our first Christmas in the farmhouse. As I worked in the kitchen on Christmas Eve, I suddenly realized that the noise level had risen dramatically. I counted noses and saw that seventeen people were gathered in the kitchen…some perched on the hearth of the Franklin fireplace, many on the table and benches Russ had built, some on the floor, and some standing.

I remember the laughter of our children when I confided that their dad was really going to love my gift to him this year. I had commissioned one of his high school friends, an artist, to paint the main street of the little town where he grew up. "It's going to be a strange Christmas," our older daughter said. When we opened gifts, I understood her comment. Russ had commissioned an artist friend to paint a picture of our farmhouse for me.

I remember the pleasure of sewing doll wardrobes on quiet evenings after the kids were in bed.

I remember the numbed feet of plowing through the snow-covered woods to cut our tree while one child kept a fearful lookout for Bigfoot and another whined that the snow had gotten inside her boots.

I remember marathons of cookie-baking for family, neighbors and friends; the satisfaction of the beautiful finished trays and the intense desire to never see another cookie for as long as I lived…or at least until next Christmas.

I remember the drives to admire the Christmas lights, with the family carsick kid (the one who got nauseous just riding to the supermarket) dividing her time between admiring the holiday decorations and throwing up in a plastic bag.

I remember Matt and I at the kitchen table after everyone else had gone to bed, furnishing and decorating the dollhouse Russ had constructed for Katy. Carols played softly on the stereo and the wind moaned around the eaves of the old house as we built balsa-wood furniture and memories.

As I relived those busy, happy years and pictured the four children who made them special, I realized that *Good Housekeeping* hadn't lied. Each of those Christmases really was "the best Christmas ever."

February, 2004

BLAH!

Usually I puzzle over why people choose to live in places like Florida, Arizona or southern California. How can they stand sweltering summers, and Christmases with whispering palms instead of crisp pines? Then this time of year arrives, and I mentally smack my forehead and mutter "Duh!" What's so great about four seasons, after all?

The problem is that we don't have four seasons here, we have five: Spring, Summer, Autumn, Winter and Blah. Blah is brownish-gray, and lasts for what feels like eternity. Sometimes there's a sunshine break for several days, maybe even a week, but you know Blah will return. If there was snow, it's brownish-gray by now; if there wasn't snow, that's still the color of our world. You go to work in the dark and come home in the dark. Fortunately, that means that you don't notice until the weekend that your yard is brownish-gray.

Sometimes I get depressed during Blah, but I don't mention it to my husband. I did once. He invited me to break the monotony by attending a work-related conference on death and dying with him. I got the feeling he missed the whole point of our conversation.

It was worse when the children were small. With four kids and the long incubation period of some illnesses, it was possible to be housebound from Christmas to Easter with chickenpox. Even worse was the combination stomach/ear/throat/sinus infection that was characterized by children whining through their stuffed-up noses all day, and needing an emergency bath and change of pajamas and sheets in the dead of night. The doctor usually diagnosed it as a virus, untreatable by antibiotic.

I often thought that if nothing could be prescribed for the children, something should be prescribed for the caretaker…preferably something with mood-altering effects. I remember hanging up on my own mother once, when I called her to whine and she told me that someday I would look back on these as the best years of my life.

Now during Blah I can curl up with a pot of tea and a good book, or computer, or sewing machine. But Blah is still there, waiting to creep in from the shadows. I get out nursery catalogs and order exotic seeds that, come planting time in April, give me a severe case of "What Was I Thinking?" syndrome. I hang out at the plant and flower department at Safeway, lingering over the pots of hyacinths until the Muzak version of "Don't Cry for Me, Argentina" is interrupted by a "Clean-up in flowers" message over the intercom. Then I know that my drooling has become a safety hazard, and I slip away, out into the brownish-gray Blah.

If Blah hangs on too long, I line the windowsills in the spare room with trays of little peat pots planted with more flower seeds than our yard can possibly accommodate. One year I used grow-lights and misted the little pots of sleeping asters, sweet peas, and marigolds twice a day. The paint peeled off the windowsills, the windows were steamed with moisture from mid-February to early April, and, had our next-door neighbors been distrustful, we might have been reported as suspected marijuana growers.

As depressing as Blah is, it's better than the horrid cold snap we had at the farm, when the pipes froze and we melted snow to flush the toilet. A big bucket of snow was good for two flushes, and whoever emptied the bucket had to refill it. Family members tried to outwait each other to avoid the trip into the Arctic tundra. We learned that teenagers have greater bladder capacity than middle-aged parents, and they rarely had to scoop snow. We showered at the firehouse across the pasture, and ice formed on wet hair during the dash home. After a suicidal cow managed to damage the wire of the electric tank heater without going to that Big Pasture in the Sky, frequent treks into the frozen north had to be made to break the ice with a hatchet. Watching ice begin to re-form as cows ambled slowly to the water tank, it was easy to see why more advanced life forms like polar bears, seals and the lichen on rocks flourish in the Arctic, while cows do not. When the pipes finally thawed, the swish of the washing machine and dishwasher, and the gurgle of water down the pipes from both showers, sounded more beautiful than a symphony.

That memory of a frozen winter has done me more good than a trip to Arizona. There are worse things than Blah…things like frostbite and snow-blindness. I guess I can outlast Blah one more time.

February, 2004

POOR, POOR PITIFUL MOM

Did it ever occur to you that there might be a few flaws in the motherhood job description? We take care of disgustingly sick people for years, but who the heck takes care of us when the germ has worked its evil way through the whole family and finally ends up in mom's body? We've cooked each child's favorite comfort food: custard topped with a spoonful of raspberry jelly; chicken broth with teensy little dumplings; green jello with marshmallows; and a trip to the store for popsicles for the child who isn't tempted by anything from the kitchen. Then we get sick and there's nothing but flat soda because somebody forgot to put the lid back on the bottle, and soda crackers that have no snap left because the vaporizer had a greater effect on them than it did on the snuffly kids. You're pretty sure you've got a high fever, but one of the kids got bored during the final day of recuperation, and took the temperature of a cup of very hot tea. With no thermometer, all you can do is lay the back of your own hand on your forehead and make an educated guess.

You expect this one-sided arrangement when kids are small. Giving alcohol sponge baths and changing sheets and pajamas in the middle of the night are just parts of the package.

At around four or five, children become full of caring and sympathy, bringing Mommy glasses of chlorine-tasting water that she sincerely hopes came from the kitchen faucet, even as she realizes that they can't reach the kitchen faucet. They pry her eyelids up with their pudgy little fingers to tell her the TV remote is lost.

This caring tends to fade in the pre-teen years. You leave work early with what feels like terminal flu, hear the kids arrive from school and think gratefully that when they bring you tea and aspirin, you'll be able to give them motherly words of wisdom before following the white light into the tunnel. They clump down the hall, fling your bedroom door open and ask, "What's for snack?" You bitterly remember all those times you played Old Maid with recuperating children, letting them win.

Finally they're old enough to take care of themselves and you can be sick with a clear conscience. You come home from work with chills and fever, turn the electric blanket to "Sauté," put on a flannel nightgown and pause at your bedroom door for a few last words. You tell them to call 911 if you're not out in three days, and to disturb you only if the house is on fire...a really big fire, not just some little kitchen blaze.

For the next couple of days you emerge only to go to the bathroom, where you see that dirty clothes are spontaneously reproducing, spilling out of the hamper onto the floor. You know you should venture into the kitchen, but just the thought brings on a relapse.

Eventually you realize that you've cheated death once more. You wander into the kitchen in search of tea, and see that a major disaster took place in your absence. A pizza box and hard crusts spill out of the garbage receptacle. Stale grease in the skillet tells you that they cooked hamburgers...many times. You'll need an SOS pad for the stove-top, and a sharp instrument to scrape the kitchen floor. You know the people who created this mess are intelligent. The kids are on the honor roll, and their father has a Master's degree. The children are flesh of your flesh, so you can't doubt their origins, but you wonder if their father was raised by wolves, and turned loose on the edge of town to prevent inbreeding within the pack.

You decide to skip the tea, and shuffle back to bed over a carpet of dirty laundry. It can wait until tomorrow, when you'll surely be stronger. You'll take advantage of one more day of rest, but it won't be time wasted. You'll be busy drawing up job descriptions for your husband and children. And somewhere in *their* document will be a bold-type, underlined section titled, "Take care of sick people."

March, 2004

THE FIRST READING LESSON

I think I'm a voracious reader because I'm still trying to make up for the time I lost by learning to read late. By third grade, I'd lost count of how many schools I'd attended. I hadn't been in one place long enough to master "See Dick. See Jane. See Spot run."

Then we moved in with an aunt and uncle, and I started attending a small country school with my two cousins. On the first day I realized that I was the only one in the whole class who didn't know how to read. The teacher gave me a note to take home. "Your mother and I need to talk about your reading problem," she explained.

I showed my cousins the note, and confessed that I didn't know how to read. Nothing fazed Hazel, a year older. "Heck, we can teach you," she assured me. "Can't we, Dorothy?" Dorothy wasn't so sure, but Hazel could bulldoze over anyone. "We'll need a book," she said confidently. "Dorothy, you go talk to the teacher so she won't see me steal one." I'm sure the teacher would have happily loaned us a book, but Hazel wouldn't have enjoyed that nearly as much as stealing one. So Dorothy occupied the teacher with lame questions while Hazel plucked a book from the shelf just inside the classroom door, and I sat waiting on a playground swing, frozen in mortal dread that the teacher would learn that not only was I dumb, but I came from a family of thieves.

Once home, we quickly did our after-school chores and took the book out behind the barn. In later times Hazel would take us behind the barn to show us that smoking weeds wrapped in toilet paper was every bit as sophisticated as smoking a real cigarette, as long as you didn't burn the barn down. She also convinced us that since we didn't have a horse, riding a cow would be just as much fun. It involved a lot of chasing but almost no riding, and when my uncle found out that it was our fault the cows stopped giving milk, our rodeo days were over. But for now, teaching an ignorant cousin how to read from a stolen book was exciting enough.

I must have been very ready to learn. After one sounding-out words session with the cousins I was able to read the book myself.

Then we went into the barn and I read the labels and instructions from sacks of chicken and cow feed, to prove I hadn't just memorized *The Corner Cat* the first time through.

I threw away the note from the teacher. Next morning we slipped the stolen book back into place and when reading class came, I volunteered to read aloud. Afterward, the teacher looked at me suspiciously and said she didn't need to meet with Mama after all, and my reading career began.

I became locally famous as the only child allowed to ride in the bookmobile. The driver would take pity on me and drop me and my armful of books off at our house on the way back to town. And if I approached the check-out desk with adult books, and the bookmobile was empty of witnesses and the books were deemed "clean and suitable" by the checker, she would let me take them.

I kept books stashed behind furniture and in the piano bench, for use while I was supposed to be doing housework. I could sneak in several pages before Mom came to find out why sweeping, or bed-making, or dusting was taking so long. In summertime I climbed the walnut tree and read in peace, hidden by the leaves. When Mom's calls became frantic, I waited until she went back inside and then climbed down and innocently reported for KP duty.

As my own children came along, story-time began when they were barely old enough to point to the pictures while I gave them the *Reader's Digest* condensed version of the story. My older daughter remembers coffee breath being one of her favorite nostalgic smells from childhood. She explained that I usually had a cup of coffee while I read to them, and the aroma of coffee drifted out with the words of the *Frances* books, and *Little House in the Big Woods*, and *Pippi Longstocking.*

I had to stop and think about that. In the books I've read, it's usually the scent of the mother's glamorous perfume that carries an adult back to childhood. Coffee breath?

I guess it could be worse. It could be that smell of burned vegetables just before the smoke alarm goes off. I'll settle for coffee breath.

June, 2004

WHAT IS IT ABOUT THE YOUNGEST KID?

I've been thinking a lot about family legends. Is the youngest child of the family the star of so many horror stories simply because his older siblings can remember and embroider on his exploits, or is it because he really *is* naughtier than everybody else?

In our family, Shawn's ability to run like a greyhound, climb like a chimpanzee and disappear like Houdini, often performing all those feats during a single five-minute time span, made us shake our heads in amazement. He quickly learned to wriggle under the stair safety gate. After I found him sitting sideways on the top step, happily swinging his legs out into space between the stair rails, I did some reinforcement. Chicken wire would have been best, but it was just too ugly. As I bought yards of nylon net, the fabric store clerk asked if I was making a prom dress for my daughter. "No," I replied. "I'm making a safety net for my son." Russ nailed the net to the rails up the side of the stairs. It took Shawn just two minutes rip the netting off the bottom nails and wriggle under, then scramble to the top of the stairs. He hadn't yet learned to walk, but he was great at scrambling.

Of course, his exploits seemed worse because I had less energy by the time he came along. I couldn't run as fast or climb as high, and he got away with more than the other kids. Or so they said.

When I was growing up, my little brother was the subject of our legends. My sister and I realize it wasn't because we were so good, it was just that he was so very bad. Our father certainly didn't have to re-seed part of the football field because WE did wheelies in the end zone after a game!

My husband was youngest by a decade, so his brother and sister had a good supply of tales. Now that they're gone, it's my duty to carry on oral history.

When he was four, Russ brought drama to a shopping trip. Following the family out of a large department store in downtown

Portland, he lagged behind, staring at the sights. When he looked up and saw that his big brother was almost through the revolving door, he put on a burst of speed, darting through as it closed. Unfortunately, it closed on his head. And it only moved clockwise. Pedestrian traffic came to a halt as people struggled to rescue the gawking little sightseer. Finally a clerk grabbed a jar of Pond's cold cream from cosmetics, greased the side of his head, and eased it back through. Russ's brother loved telling the story of the "only kid dumb enough to get his head stuck in a revolving door."

His sister described how at age five, he decided to nail together two boards while sitting on the kitchen floor. He missed the nail and hit his thumb. He yelled "Jesus..." and saw his mother and sister stop what they were doing, turn and frown at him. Without missing a beat, he gazed piously at the ceiling and sang, "loves me, this I know."

Growing up in tiny Klickitat, he always came home from school for lunch. Once in third grade his mother wasn't home. He ignored the sandwich she had left, preferring toast. Making the first two slices was so much fun that he toasted and buttered the remainder of the loaf. Then, realizing he was in trouble, he covered the stack with a tablecloth and went back to school. (He never claimed to be the brightest bulb in the chandelier.)

At about the same age Russ shot his long-suffering father in the neck with his new BB gun, testing to see how distance affected aim. His grown brother and sister were amazed that Russ's punishment was just a good scolding and confiscation of his gun for a week.

In fourth grade he rolled the family's brand-new empty oil barrel into the Klickitat River to see if it would float. It did, right on out to the Columbia, and probably the Pacific Ocean. Since their house was next to the river, he didn't get tired out when he threw most of the woodpile into the water, piece by piece. He explained he'd done it so the campers downstream would have enough wood for their fires. His siblings suspected he just enjoyed throwing stuff in the river.

Come to think of it, Shawn wasn't misbehaving so badly when he scaled the stairs like King Kong. It could have been worse. At least he never shot his father in the neck. And luckily, we didn't live near a river.

July, 2004

LET'S HAVE A PICNIC!

When I was a kid I loved picnics, and couldn't understand why Mom gave a long sigh each time Dad said brightly, on the way home from church, "Let's go on a picnic!" Then I became the picnic-packer, and I knew why she sighed.

The carefree little jaunt means loading boxes with hot food that you wrap in towels in a vain attempt to keep hot, and cold food that you pack in ice to avoid food poisoning. Then you add the simple things that are always within close reach in the kitchen: salt, pepper, mustard, catsup, yellow-jacket spray…that kind of stuff. Next comes a tablecloth, and four large rocks to hold down the cloth so it won't blow into the next county (which, by the way, is never a problem back home in your well-equipped kitchen).

After loading the car and making a couple of trips back into the house for important things you've forgotten, the family finally sets out for their favorite park, where you find the good spots are already taken. So you make the hike from parking lot to a distant table, with everyone in the family drafted into pack-mule duty. One child usually manages to drag the tablecloth through the dirt, and the one carrying the cake or pie quite often drops it. And of course it never lands right side up.

When everyone finally settles at the picnic table, you learn why it was one of the few unoccupied sites. It's the all-you-can-eat buffet location for yellow-jackets. You spray liberally, hoping to kill the invaders without poisoning your family. Everyone eats cautiously, checking each bite for wasps before putting it in the mouth.

The climax to a perfect picnic is the unexpected rain shower. The covered areas were snatched up by smarter picnic-goers early on, so the only recourse is to eat as fast as possible without swallowing a yellow-jacket. You haul all the stuff back to the car and head home, where you put everything away. After carefully scraping off the ants, you put food back in the cupboard or refrigerator. The tablecloth goes in the laundry, the crusty eating utensils are put to soak, and the curtain falls on another Kodak moment.

After I had a family of my own and learned that for the mom, picnics are more fun than camping trips only because they don't last as long, I continued to willingly pack those boxes. Why? Because of a few childhood picnics that still linger in my memory.

The best was Dad's after-church inspiration to have a picnic at the beach, about two hours away. Mom grabbed some food she had planned to fix for lunch, filled a big Thermos with coffee, and we were off. By the time we got there, a misty rain was falling. The wind felt like it was coming in off the Arctic Ocean, not the Pacific, but after driving that far, we were not going to be denied our picnic. Dad piled driftwood for a wind barrier, brought a utility tarp from the car and secured it with more driftwood to make a lean-to shelter, and built a roaring fire at the mouth of the lean-to.

I know there must have been a nutritious lunch, but that's not what I remember. I remember rye bread and home-churned butter, sharp Cheddar cheese, and Mom's homemade pear marmalade. I tried for years to replicate that sweet, citrusy, linger-on-your-taste-buds jam but mine was never as good. Maybe it was because I wasn't washing down the rye bread and marmalade with the rare grown-up treat of coffee from a Thermos. Or maybe nothing tastes as good at the kitchen table as it did with the family gathered by the fire in a cozy lean-to, hearing the wind howl and the waves crash.

I'm sure that none of the picnics I packed for my own family compared to that childhood memory, but I still haven't given up. Now the favorites of the grandchildren are included in the menu, and dessert has to be chocolate, for the chocoholic grandkids. I use a lot of labor-saving devices Mom didn't have access to, like buying a bucket of KFC instead of frying chicken in the big iron skillet. The potato salad I pick up at the deli isn't as good as her homemade salad was, but I skip the chopping, slicing and dicing. If I'm feeling fancy, I might transfer it from the carton to my own dish so nobody knows I took the lazy way out.

But some parts of the old-time picnic don't change. We'll still haul our boxes and baskets across the parking lot. Somebody will trail the tablecloth in the dirt. And when the cake is dropped, it still lands upside-down.

July, 2004

THE SCOFIELD CURSE

Most families have traditions, and ours is no exception. It's just a shame they're not pretty.

We have the legend of the Scofield Vacation Curse...family trips that become entertaining stories only after enough time has passed to dull memory.

Driving through Los Angeles freeway traffic in August at rush hour with an overheated radiator and no exit in sight became a tale of valor. Somebody remembered reading that turning off the air conditioner and running the heater was helpful. Those in the front seat rode with their feet on the dash to avoid the blasting inferno. We lowered all the windows, strangled on exhaust and wished we had a St. Christopher figurine hanging from the mirror. But even that wouldn't have been strong enough to defeat the Curse.

The Scofield Vacation Curse was active on our trip to the World's Fair in Spokane. The two older kids had weekend jobs and couldn't go, for which they were later grateful. Shawn hadn't been feeling too perky, but he said he was much better, and well enough to go. Since he had a tendency to be dubiously sick on school days and get well for the weekend, we didn't doubt him, and set off.

The hotels and motels were packed, but we had finally found reservations in what was described as a "grand old Victorian mansion, made into a guest house." Maybe it had been grand at one time...long, long ago. Behind the bathtub was a hole in the wall, out of which swarmed tiny black flying insects. We used adhesive tape from our first-aid kit to fasten a "Welcome to Spokane" brochure over the hole, and the temporary patch lasted through the first two showers. It was midnight and there was no place to go, so we closed the bathroom door and prayed the little critters wouldn't fly through the keyhole.

Next morning both kids looked a little pale, but they swore they felt fine. We had breakfast at Denny's, making a hasty exit when Shawn needed fresh air. At the Fair we battled lines and saw exhibits, but the two youngsters weren't as lively as usual. We decided to put the kids on the gondola for a relaxing trip around the park, while we rested and Russ battled a worsening headache. "We'll wait right here," I called cheerfully as their gondola car swung away.

Time passed, and they didn't return. Worried, I went to the hospitality booth manned by two gentle nuns and reported that our children hadn't returned from the around-the-park gondola ride. "Around the park?" one said. "My dear, that ride is ACROSS the park…one-way. They have to buy a return ticket at the other end."

We knew the kids didn't have money for a return ticket. Besides, their older sister and brother usually took care of things like that, and although Shawn and Katy were eight and nine years old, they probably wouldn't have known how to buy tickets. Russ got on the gondola to retrieve his lost children, while I stayed put in case they somehow found their way back. More time passed, and finally I reported to the hospitality booth again, saying that now my husband was lost, too. The two nuns were less gentle this time, and I could tell they were re-thinking the birth control question; that maybe in some cases it might have been a good idea.

I set off on foot, looking up to follow the gondola route as closely as possible. I had to detour around obstacles, which meant I sometimes lost view of it. I reached the boundary of the park without seeing my family pass overhead, and walked back. I headed for the hospitality booth to ask if any visitors had been taken away in ambulances, and joyfully saw my husband and children waiting on a bench by the door. They had gone to inquire about ME, and the nuns wouldn't let them leave.

We took turns driving and moaning on the way home, both adults sick. We visited every rest stop, finally parking in one for a few hours when we were both too ill to continue.

You'd think the trip itself should have been punishment enough, but oh, no! The final blow came when Shawn wrote about it for a class project, and his teacher read it to me at parent conference. She gave me a measuring gaze that resembled the ones I'd received from the nuns at the hospitality booth, cleared her throat, and began.

"I'd been sick," my little turncoat had written, "but Mom said the tickets were hard to get, so we went to the World's Fair anyhow. We had lots of bugs in our hotel room. Mom and Dad put my sister and me on a one-way ride….."

The Curse still lives, years later. We just try not to think about it.

August, 2004

MATT'S RED CONVERTIBLE

We're finally putting Matt's red convertible up for sale. We thought we were ready twice before, but realized at the last minute that we couldn't bear to see a stranger drive off behind the wheel of our son's car.

He found his dream car at a lot on South First Street. He needed a co-signer and Dad was at work, so Matt came home and got me. "Are you out of your mind?" I asked, always practical. "You buy old cheese or old wine, not old cars!"

Matt would have had a much easier time of it if his dad hadn't been at work. Men seem to have an unexplainable streak of insanity when it comes to cars. "But it's a collector's item," Matt protested. "It's insanity!" I replied. "You need a 1969 red Mercury Cougar convertible like you need another hole in your head. Antique is fine for furniture, not cars!"

Eventually he wore me down, and drove us out of the car lot onto South First Street, where the hood flew up, stranding us in traffic. "I thought that thirty-day warrantee was bad, but thirty minutes? Give me a break!" Matt said, hopping out to close the hood.

How Matt loved that car. When I close my eyes I see him tanned and healthy, vibrant with life, polishing it to a candy-apple red glow in the shade of the big fir tree on the farm. A high-school friend remembers driving with him over Snoqualmie Pass to a concert in Seattle. They left the top down, and sang at the top of their lungs as the snow whitened their hair. I'm grateful she told me about this adventure much later. The mother in me associates that kind of activity with fiery plunges off mountain peaks.

Matt left for California in his red convertible at the age of nineteen, setting out with the supreme confidence that comes with the naiveté of youth.

Seven years later we drove down and towed our dead son's car back home. In Matt's struggle to live, the convertible had been neglected. A fender was crumpled. Someplace in East L.A., the top had been slashed. Smog had done ugly things to the candy-apple glow.

We rented a truck to bring back our son's possessions…the furniture he had saved money to buy, the books and music he loved, his clothing. On the floor of his closet I found a shirt meant for the laundry. Holding it to my face, I breathed in the scent of cedar, soap and skin that was my son. I saw him leaping off a bus and walking to his house, jacket thrown over his shoulder and shirtsleeves rolled to the elbow, breathing in the atmosphere of that multi-cultured city he loved so much. I sealed the shirt in plastic to preserve the scent, and have it still.

When we left L.A., our last stop was at the home of the Guerrero family. Their daughter, Gloria, was Matt's co-worker when he first arrived in California, and they became his second family. He spent holidays with them when he couldn't make it home…helped the little nieces carve pumpkins and dye Easter eggs, attended confirmations and family birthday parties. Mrs. Guerrero spoke little English and I spoke no Spanish, but we managed. She came from the kitchen with a foil-wrapped dish and placed it in my hands. "Is last time I send our Mateo's tamales home," she said brokenly, through tears.

Back home, we parked the convertible in a shed until we were strong enough to deal with it. When that time finally came, our mechanic son-in-law rebuilt the engine and carburetor, and did all the other things Matt's beloved car needed. A body shop straightened the fender and pounded out dents. We bought a new top, and had the convertible painted its original candy-apple red. When everything was completed, we bought a new license plate bearing the word "Memory."

The car hasn't been driven many miles since then. Russ drove our granddaughter's Camp Fire group in it for a Naches Sportsman's Days parade, and the occasional politician waved from it in SunFair parades.

Our younger daughter bought me a "riding in the convertible" straw hat that ties under the chin with a wide red ribbon, and for Russ, a white cap with a brim that shades his eyes from the sun. We haven't worn them much. On our first sentimental ride, I could almost hear Matt chuckling gently at the sight of his gray-haired mom and dad tooling down Yakima Avenue in his bright red convertible.

Our one-car garage holds a car that seldom leaves it, so we're going to do the sensible thing and sell it. But when it pulls out of our driveway with a stranger behind the wheel, I won't be watching. I'll have the volume turned high while I listen to some of Matt's music, so I won't hear the throaty roar of the car. And I'll be seeing our son giving us a confident wave as he sets off for his future in that candy-apple red convertible.

September, 2004

THE ANIMAL KINGDOM

Our kids always had pets, ranging from mindless goldfish to lovable dogs.

They all went through the aquarium phase, where you start with crystal water and darting tetra, and, after boredom sets in, end with thick, cloudy water and whichever fish is bred for survival. Of course each child went through the phase separately, which meant that for many years I periodically found remnants of smelly gravel in my kitchen sink after the aquarium was cleaned. Near the end of each child's aquarium adventure the gravel in the sink occurred much less frequently than it had at the beginning, but it still happened too often.

The turtle didn't have even as much personality as the fish. It was so sluggish we never knew if it was just sleeping soundly, or dead. The lettuce bits browned, the grapes withered, and still we couldn't decide. Finally, when an evil smell came from the shell, we gave it the traditional shoebox funeral.

Then there was the chameleon that escaped the cage. It probably became dessert for the cat, but for as long as we lived in that house I never got up in the night without a pang of terror as my feet touched the floor.

Birds were a bit more personable than fish. Matt had a parakeet that he was sure would learn to talk with enough training and repetition. He bought a book and tape at the pet store, and for an entire summer the house echoed with "Pret-ty bird. Pret-ty bird." Tweetie never learned to say the phrase, but it clanged in the brains of the rest of us.

Tweetie's cage was in the kitchen. Although he never said "pret-ty bird", he struggled to be louder than any competing noise, such as the radio, dishwasher, or casual conversation. I had sewed a cage cover to keep him warm at night, and Tweetie lived a strange schedule which sometimes had as many as a dozen nights in a twenty-four-hour period.

We loved our dogs fiercely, regardless of personality quirks, smell or lack of intelligence (the dog's, not ours).

A friend gave us a German Shepherd who seemed perfectly normal. A month later she became ill, and the vet delivered eleven stillborn puppies. Home again, she developed what must have been postpartum psychosis. She attached herself to one child and became Cujo to the rest of us. She spent the days dragging around a tee-shirt her hero had left on his bedroom floor, resting with her head on it. When I tried to retrieve it for the laundry, she growled menacingly and the fur on her neck stood up. When I entered her master's room in the morning to wake him for school, she rose, growling gutturally, fangs bared, from the side of his bed where she had spent the night on guard. The child possessing all this power enjoyed it, but we finally found the dog a home where viciousness was an asset. There really is such a trait as "mean as a junkyard dog."

Then there was Goldie, who appointed herself the official mascot of the volunteer fire department across the pasture. When the fire-hall was built, Russ decided that as long as he was going to wake up every time the siren blew, he might as well join. Goldie joined too, sitting by his chair at every meeting, trying to catch the water when they practiced with hoses.

Goldie made one think that the jokes about the IQ of blondes might have some basis in fact. In addition to trying to catch water, she hopped in the car with anyone who opened the door. Since the fire-hall parking lot was a late-night teenage gathering place, she encountered many open doors. She'd been missing a week when a neighbor called and said he'd seen our dog trying to catch water in front of a fire-hall in town. The firemen were sorry to see Goldie go when Russ picked her up. They'd already bought a sack of kibble and a comfy bed since she'd wandered in a few days earlier.

Stray cats and dogs had a way of ending up at our house. I think the animal word was out that a real softie lived there…Russ. I looked out the kitchen window once and saw him headed for the alfalfa field to move irrigation pipes. The cat waited, as always, on the gatepost, and leaped to his shoulder when he paused. He made quite a picture with an irrigation pipe on one shoulder, the cat on the other, followed by two dogs and a frolicking lamb who could leap any fence on the place. She never ran away, though. An orphan lamb who had been fed from a nursing bottle, she thought she was one of our children.

Our grown kids keep saying Dad needs a dog. I'll remind them again: the days of gravel in the sink and hair on the furniture are long gone. Besides, our cat would chase even Cujo off the place.

September, 2004

AND I THOUGHT THE SUPERMARKET WAS BAD!

I just got back from Costco and hauled all that stuff into the house. There wasn't cupboard space for everything, of course, even after I put all the cleaning and paper supplies out in the garage. Glancing at the far wall, I realized I had enough toilet paper to TP the front yard of every popular football player at Yakima high schools. And there are so many economy size packages of paper towels stored out there that I could probably give up cloth towels entirely, and still have enough paper ones to last until the kids cart me off to Shady Pines.

Back in the house, I began cramming cans and packages on shelves. Russ has installed two additional cabinets in the kitchen, but they're full, too. The other day I was making soup and asked our daughter to get me two cans of tomatoes. She looked at me strangely when I directed her to the hallway coat closet. What's the big deal? There's a good two feet of space left on the floor under the coats…perfect for storing cases of canned goods.

I think when I enter Costco, I'm channeling the spirit of someone who starved in a Biblical famine. I see those fantastic prices on giant quantities and I'm hooked. So what if I'm cooking for two, not two hundred? Who cares if none of my shelves are tall enough to hold a gallon bottle of olive oil? The price is right.

Sometimes I worry I might be out of control…like when I boil and refrigerate the last half of the bag of tiny red potatoes because they're starting to trail green sprouts. Two people don't eat that many potatoes, but they're such cute little things, and so much cheaper than in a store.

When I throw away part of the ready-to-serve salad mix because it expired right when the date on the bag said it would, I feel guilty. I remember all those times Mom told us to eat our vegetables because there were children starving in China. But as I finally realized at about the age of eight, there was no way to send my uneaten vegetables to

China, so why worry? Even if I use only half the bag of salad, it's still cheaper to buy it in bulk.

I've tried to avoid temptation by sending my husband with a list, but that doesn't work too well. Last time he came home with a gallon of teriyaki marinade. Even if we barbecue all winter in our parkas and snow boots, we'll never use it up. I've marinated everything but his oatmeal, and barely changed the level in the jar. The only thing I haven't tried is teriyaki meatballs…the product they were giving out samples of when they hooked him. To do that I'd have to buy one of those gigantic bags of meatballs. With all my brain-power invested in dreaming up ways to use meatballs *and* teriyaki marinade, bad things would happen. I'd probably forget to take my daily dose of Senior Moments, the "advanced memory-enhancing dietary supplement" our daughter gave me for Christmas.

Of course, there has to be a drawback to scoring these bargains. In this case, the drawback is people…many, many people. Some of them are families who evidently make the Costco trip their weekly entertainment outing with the kids. Instead of burgers and a movie, the outing consists of hitting all the free samples, then congregating in the aisles displaying books, DVDs, and CDs.

Then there are the folks who run into neighbors, park their carts head-to-head across the aisle, and enjoy a long chat. At times like this I have to remind myself that even my father, a bit of a curmudgeon, didn't make rude hand gestures in crowded stores. Nor did he back up and make a running charge with a loaded cart, as I fight the urge to do.

But the man who hauled heavy hods of bricks for a dollar a day in the Depression; who worked hard on water biscuits, water gravy and beans, would love Costco. When Dad finally had a farm of his own he tilled gardens far larger than we could use, and Mom canned and froze it all, to his immense satisfaction and security. If Dad were still living, he'd have built an extra room for storage after filling the garage.

Hey, I'll bet it's not a Biblical famine victim I'm channeling! Maybe it's my own father. It would explain more than my bulging cupboards. It would also explain that urge to back up and make a running charge, scattering carts like bowling pins!

October, 2004

IS SHE HER BROTHER'S KEEPER?

Often our children looked out for one another as they were growing up, but there were many times when I reflected that if they were depending on each other to be brother's keepers, our kids were in a whole lot of trouble.

When they were small, our older daughter Luanne was protective of Matt, two years younger. During a kids-only visit to Grandma's house, Matt did something naughty and Grandma gave him a swat on the behind. Four-year-old Luanne glared at Grandma, grabbed Matt and took him into the bedroom. She emerged a few minutes later, leading her brother and dragging their suitcase, a pajama leg hanging out one side. "We're going home now," she told Grandma angrily. "Our mom and dad wouldn't want someone being mean to Matt!" She struggled to get the front door open and they marched up the sidewalk toward the main street of tiny Klickitat. Grandma explained later that she peeked from behind the curtains to see if she needed to run after them, but it wasn't necessary. Luanne knew she wasn't supposed to cross the street by herself, so they stood on the corner for a lo-o-ong time. Finally they came back. "It's getting dark," Luanne informed Grandma. "We'll go tomorrow morning instead."

I thought maybe the older sister was always protective, but I learned that isn't the case. Our third and fourth children, Katrina and Shawn, came along some years later, like a second little family. It was plain to see that Katy would have been happy to remain the youngest child. "Brother's Keeper" was not in her job description.

Our old farmhouse had a big kitchen with a brick hearth and Franklin fireplace, and when I worked there I would bring the playpen in, fill it with toys and put baby Shawn inside, while Katy sat on the hearth with her stack of Little Golden Books. Shawn would throw out all the toys, shriek and shake the bars. All he needed was a tin cup to rattle against them to equal a scene from a stereotypical prison movie. Finally I'd set him free, at which time Katy slung her entire Little Golden library into the playpen and crawled over the bars to solitude. Then Shawn stood outside and shook the bars, howling to get back in.

From the time he learned to walk, Shawn ran. I'm sure that during the time the child was under my watchful gaze, he was planning in detail exactly what he was going to do next, so he wouldn't waste valuable time when freedom came. Our farmhouse was a long way back from the road. I'd take the two toddlers outside and mend or write letters while they played. When I had to go in to get different thread or more paper, it was always a rush trip. He *had* to have his plan already developed in order to cover so much space in so little time.

Once I ran out and he was gone. I frantically asked Katy where her brother was, and she gave a nonchalant wave toward the highway. When I snatched him off the yellow line and marched him back down the driveway, he told me he was going to "the 'tore." The store was about two miles away, but he was headed in the right direction. In a severe, self-righteous tone Katy said she had *told* him to stay in the yard. I still wonder.

They were in high school the first time Katy was truly protective of her younger brother. At the end of his unfortunate, knot-head, drinking-at-a-school-dance experiment, she and a friend dumped him in the car, stuck his head out the window and drove miles of country roads with the cold March wind blowing in his face. They stopped several times to pour 7-11 coffee down his throat, and came home when she thought he'd be able to negotiate the stairs to his room. We heard the back door slam, but by the time we got to the hallway they were near the top of the stairs, Katy closely behind her brother. "G'night, Mom! G'night, Dad!" she called over her shoulder cheerfully.

Of course Shawn got busted, big-time, when the principal called next morning. After hanging up, their dad summoned the two kids. "Why on earth did you pick this time, of all times, to protect your brother?" I demanded of Katy. She looked me straight in the eye and said unapologetically, "Well, I thought he was too young to die."

The kids all learned to love and accept each other by the time they were grown, but often I sincerely hoped there was backup manpower in the "Brother's Keeper" department. In baseball terms, they frequently needed a pinch- hitter. Being your brother's keeper is a big job.

November 2004

COULD BE AS EFFECTIVE AS THE PILL

When we learned that our older daughter and her husband didn't plan to have children, I blamed myself. I figured she'd had all the caretaking she could stand with her younger siblings.

I remembered the summer she was fourteen, and babysat while I had a summer job. Driving home from work one day, I saw cars slowing down in front of our house, and people gawking and pointing. Three-year-old Shawn was tied to a tree in the front yard, where he had perfected looking pitiful into an art form. I untied him and rushed him into the house, hoping a passerby hadn't already called Child Protective Services.

Luanne was too tired to pretend remorse. "He's safer this way," she declared. "When I tried to keep him inside, he pulled a chair to the door and climbed up to unlock the screen. When I let him outside, he ran away every time my back was turned. So I finally tied him up. The rope was around his waist, not his neck, and he could move around. He was in the shade. He had cold water, and Popsicles, and everything Fisher-Price ever made!"

I recalled another incident when Shawn was about four. The third time he did something I'd told him not to, I swatted him lightly on the behind. Clutching his offended bottom, he spun around and yelled, "You're just a mean old Mama!" A completely uninvolved Luanne entered the room, and he shouted at her, "And you are, too!"

Good grief, no wonder she didn't want children.

She was more than just a duty-driven big sister. There was that time she spent part of a Saturday tearing up newspapers and mixing them with wallpaper paste to make paper maché. With the paper maché and colored tissue she created an elaborate piñata for her little sister's birthday party.

And how about that tree-house she helped Shawn build? Actually, his part consisted mostly of carrying scrap lumber from the barn to the willow tree and handing it up to his big sister, and hammering in nails when the project was far enough along that it was safe for him to be aloft. But she made him feel like he had built it.

Probably the best example of big sister duty occurred once when Russ and I had a rare evening out. The two younger kids were in their early teens, so we felt it was safe to leave them home alone. When we drove into the carport after the movie, I thought I smelled smoke. Russ told me it was my imagination. We had just seen "Carrie," in which the teenager who doesn't have a good time at the prom ends the evening by burning the entire town.

We entered a kitchen cleaner than I'd seen it since we moved in. The walls and even the ceiling sparkled. But strangely, the window had no curtains. Their charred remnants were in the backyard, where they'd been flung in the firefighting. Katy, Shawn and Luanne sagged in exhaustion at the kitchen table.

In a rare act of sisterly love (or boredom), Katy had decided to make french fries for her brother. She put the skillet of oil on the burner to heat, then got side-tracked by TV until they heard a giant "whoosh" from the kitchen. They poured salt and soda on the burning oil, dunked the flaming curtains in the sink and threw them outside, and put out the spot fires on the cupboard doors. Then they called big sister for help. Luanne was married and in her own home by this time, and probably thought her days of rescuing siblings were finally finished, but she came to their aid. They spent three hours scrubbing smoke-stained walls and ceilings.

So I couldn't blame Luanne for deciding to be childless. We sold the baby furniture and Fisher-Price toys at a yard sale. When they later decided to have children after all, I was so grateful I didn't even mind replacing all the stuff. After all, what would life be without grandkids? Remembering all the hours and energy Luanne gave her younger siblings, I've tried to return the favor with her two children.

Oh, who am I kidding? I'm not being noble. I just do it because it's fun! Luckily, I've never had to tie either of them to a tree.

November, 2004

THANKSGIVING IN THE NORTHWEST RAIN FOREST

Back before we got sensible and said families with four children should spend the holidays in their own home, and not trail around like a traveling circus, we did the "taking turns" thing. One year it'd be Thanksgiving with Russ's family and Christmas with mine, and the next year the order was reversed. Truthfully, I think both families breathed a sigh of relief when we said that from now on, we'd welcome them as guests, but the six of us were going to be like the song: "Home for the Holidays." By the time you have four kids, even their grandparents greet you with less enthusiasm than when you had just one or two.

When we spent Thanksgiving with my family, we had a tradition. (According to our younger daughter, tradition means doing something the same way twice, especially if it's something she enjoys. Traditions were formed rather quickly in this child's mind.) Like many family traditions, the individual members remember this one with varying degrees of fondness. Russ remembers it with gloom and loathing, because he was the driver. The kids loved it. As for me…I enjoy sitting in my warm, dry living room and remembering it much more than I enjoyed the actual experience.

Thanksgiving Day was the usual eating, watching parades and football on TV, and playing board games.Our traditional festivities took place the next day.

We made our way to downtown Portland, crawled through traffic until finding a place to park, and splashed out to watch the Santa Claus Parade in the pouring rain. Seeing the jolly old elf was actually our number two goal. Number one was to avoid poking someone in the eye with an umbrella, or being poked. Sometimes we just clumped together and spread a piece of plastic over our heads.

When the parade ended, we joined what seemed like half the population of Portland walking around all four block-long sides of the Meier and Frank department store to see what wonderful new mechanical Christmas scenes they'd dreamed up for the display windows.

Sensible people would have gone home to rest up for the next act of our Thanksgiving Spectacular, but we knew we'd never get Russ back in the car again if we went home. So we'd find a restaurant and eat very slowly so our clothes could get as dry as possible, after which we did some shopping (another of Russ's least-favorite activities).

Then we headed for Lloyd's Center shopping mall in Portland, which was Russ's very favorite part of the day. For some reason he associates Lloyd's Center with pounding headaches. We circled the underground parking so long that the various color level signs blended into a sickening puce. By the time we finally found a spot, the carsick kid in the back seat was hanging her head out the window, trying to stop the inevitable. Since she was breathing in exhaust, not fresh air, the inevitable usually happened even sooner.

With clothes still slightly rain-damp, we stiffly climbed out of the car, while everybody told everybody else to remember that we were parked in Level Purple. This level, we were sure, was just slightly above the area that was heated subterraneously by the fires of Hell. In fact, Russ was convinced that's where he actually was.

Unless we were near an elevator (which rarely happened) we began the climb to the surface, like weary coal miners at the end of their shift. On the earth's surface once more, we were mashed into a crowd of people who were all just as crazy as we were, watching as a lovely young lady wearing a tiara trimmed with battery-operated candles entered. (Just try explaining the Scandinavian tradition of Lucia, Queen of Light to tired kids who can't hear you over the crowd noise unless you yell.)

Then all the hardships were forgotten. She threw the switch, and the giant Christmas tree in the center of the plaza shimmered with twinkling lights. Along with everybody else, we sighed "Oooh! Aaah!"

Then we descended into the bowels of the earth, where we eventually found our car, and drove back to my parents' house for the rest of the weekend. The colds resulting from exposure usually began showing symptoms before we got back to our own home.

I nostalgically mentioned that wonderful Thanksgiving tradition to Russ the other day. He gave me a black look and took his newspaper out to the garage, slamming the back door on the way. Obviously, his memory of the tradition hasn't mellowed as much as mine has over the years. And they say time heals all wounds!

February, 2005

HARD TIMES AT THE GYM

Thank heavens the father's genes are as hardworking as the mother's, or our kids would be uncoordinated and athletically pitiful, like me.

Horrible visions from the past came thundering back to me when we recently joined an athletic club. Water exercise was recommended by my doctor, and I'm eager enough to get back to normal that I gladly signed up for water-walking, and a program for arthritis sufferers.

My progress is hampered by the fact that I'm deathly afraid of water. (Fortunately, children are no longer taught to swim by being thrown in a river. My brain told me that my father and uncles wouldn't let me drown, but when you're snorting up what feels like half the Lewis River through your nose and mouth, the brain ceases to function.) The instructor gave me two foam "noodles" to keep me afloat in case I capsize (hard to do in the shallow end of the pool, but possible).

Since we do the same exercises at each session, I tell myself that I might be able to do them correctly by the end of the classes. I'll just have to watch carefully time after time, and eventually I'll be able to do what the rest of the class is doing at the *time* they do it, not fifteen seconds later, by copying them. But I have excuses for my ineptitude. After all, the instructor is facing us, so I have to translate her left into my right. And there's that little matter of which leg and arm you start out with. On the Animal Planet channel, even animals with tiny brains stride out confidently, not worrying about which foot to place first. I tell myself that when I'm walking normally, surely I must be doing it right. But in the exercise, if you step out with your right leg, it's your left arm that's supposed to swing forward. I take a couple of steps and look down to check. Darn it, I'm swinging my right arm and leg out at the same time again. I do a quick-step to get things right and then I'm usually in step until I reach the edge, but when I start back the same thing happens. It's even worse when we're instructed to walk backward. I usually end up rapidly switching from arm to arm, thrashing around so much water that it looks like we're shooting a scene from "Jaws".

In grade school, I was always the next-to-last kid called to be on a team. Children weren't taught to be politically correct regarding the handicapped back then, or I would have been the *last* one called. The student called after me was in a wheelchair. Of course, if kindness and empathy were being taught, the big tough kid who was always best in sports wouldn't have been allowed to call out his choice of players...the teacher would have assigned them.

What was pathetic was that I couldn't even blame the leaders who didn't call me. I stood there, a skinny little kid with pigtails braided so tightly that my scalp looked like it had goose-bumps. My glasses slid down my nose constantly, and I'd developed the nervous tic of pushing them back up, even when they hadn't slid down yet. Part of me was silently willing the chooser to forget I was there, and part of me was mentally pleading, "Choose me! Choose me! I can do it right this time!" But of course I never did. Standing way out in the field, squinting up through the sun's glare at the ball approaching me, I bravely held up my cupped hands, over-sized mitt sliding around uselessly. Then at the very last minute my hands dropped to protect my face, and the ball thudded to the ground behind me. Who in their right mind would have chosen me, unless forced to?

It didn't improve in high school. The best part of P.E. field hockey was when I got hit in the nose by the ball. The swelling was gross, but it got me off the field for a few days. I sort of enjoyed badminton, but perspiration took the curl out of my hair. I loved the policy allowing us to sit out a few days a month for feminine reasons, until the P.E. teacher sent a note to my mother that I needed to see a doctor. Seems that my feminine reasons excused me about three times as often as other girls' did.

Adulthood gave me exercise of a different kind: chasing kids and runaway animals, climbing stairs. I did a lot of mall walking, but I enjoyed it only when it ended in a department store.

So now I'm back to organized sports. I'm just grateful you don't have to be chosen for a team in water-walking!

March, 2005

THUNDERING HERDS

One evening recently we were watching the Discovery channel and saw herds of wildebeest thundering across the savannah. For some reason it made me think of our years as clueless farmers. We didn't raise wildebeests, but almost every animal on our farm thundered across the pasture, through the fence, and made a beeline for the neighbor's flower garden. I could never understand why an animal chose imported Dutch iris over a field of alfalfa. I think it was the same sheer perversity that also caused other people's livestock to leave their own green pastures and head for ours.

Some of the most exciting chases involved not one of our animals, but the big Black Angus bull belonging to a neighbor. Inside that huge, scary, muscular body beat the heart of a teddy bear, but when standing between him and the highway, armed only with a broom, it was hard to remember how tame he was. And this animal was more than just future steaks and pot roasts…he was a thoroughbred bull, valuable for breeding, so keeping him off the highway was important.

A Japanese exchange student was having dinner with us one spring evening when a neighbor called to say that Ferdinand was out and headed our way. By this time we all knew our battle stations, and we surged out the back door, grabbing weapons on the way. Yoshi followed in utter confusion. The only weapon left was the dust mop, so I handed it to him. (Of course a broom or dust mop wouldn't fend off a determined bull, but we figured anything that made us look larger or more threatening had to help.) Yoshi followed Matt to his post at the end of the lane. When Ferdinand rounded the barn and sauntered up the lane, Yoshi gasped, then launched a nervous giggle that lasted until Ferdinand realized he was outnumbered and headed back to his own pasture. I'm sure that somewhere in Japan, a man entertains his children with the heroic story of how, armed only with a dust mop, he fought off a raging bull.

Chasing cattle was bad enough, but the pig escapade won the frustration prize.

I came home from work at noon to attend a Mother's Tea at the high school. As I was changing clothes, the neighbor called. "Your pig is in my flowers," she said tersely. She was a lovely eighty-four-year-old widow whose garden was her pride and joy. I think our animals sensed that, which helped them decide where to head the moment they found freedom. She was always polite, but I'm sure she privately felt she lived next door to Ma and Pa Kettle.

I threw on my robe and headed over. After much chasing, we herded the pig out of her flowers and back into our alfalfa field, where he had plenty of room for strategic maneuvers as I tried to get him into the pigpen. I chased him around the alfalfa until he finally collapsed in a sort of swine swoon. Just in case he was faking, I sat on him while he wheezed and gasped. Tearing the belt off my robe, I tied it around his neck and eventually dragged him to the pigpen, where he meekly ran back under the fence through the hole he had dug. I plugged up the hole with big rocks (easily available, since rocks were the only thing we raised successfully). After a long, hot shower, I went to the tea. I hoped I was only imagining a hint of Eau de Piggy, but just to be safe, I tried not to get too close to anyone.

I remembered my childhood on a farm, and realized that none of our current chases were as exciting as rounding up turkeys. Dad bought a dozen turkey chicks, figuring we'd keep one for Thanksgiving and one for Christmas, and sell the rest at holiday time. By the time the holidays drew near, only three were left. Turkeys are so truly stupid that they sometimes drown by tipping their heads back and opening their beaks during a hard rain. Mom took down the third turkey in October. He escaped, and she and I chased the idiot until all three of us, chasers and chasee, were gasping for breath. Sensing that he was getting his second wind, Mom made a final lunge, held out her apron as a net, and fell on him. It broke his neck, but we didn't even care. She dressed him out and we had turkey for dinner.

Thanks heavens Russ and I never tried raising turkeys. Cows and pigs were bad enough. Since I don't wear aprons, I'd be really handicapped chasing turkeys.

Now we buy our pot roasts at the supermarket. It's not as satisfying as raising our own, but it's a heck of a lot easier!

May, 2005

THEY DO REJOIN THE HUMAN RACE

You've heard of the book *Women are From Venus, Men are From Mars,* I'm sure. I always thought the title was incomplete. It should have included "...*and Adolescent Boys are from the Planet GodHelpUs*."

Our boys weren't even all that bad, according to statistics. Neither of them held up a convenience store, or mugged an old lady for her Social Security money, or dealt drugs. Of course, if they had I wouldn't have known about it until the police came knocking on the door, because of the boys' DUM policy. Years later, when I learned about the policy, they explained that it wasn't formulated to keep them from getting in trouble, but out of devotion to their mother. DUM stood for Don't Upset Mom. Our daughters probably had a similar policy, but they haven't confessed yet. I've found that although girls communicate better in their teenage years because they use actual words instead of grunts and snarls, they are also capable of being sneakier than boys.

Males' sudden transition is the thing that puzzles their mothers. One day they're fairly loveable young animals whose main faults are armpit noises, burping the alphabet and clumsily knocking lamps off end-tables. Next day they're moody, snarling beasts who shower three times a day, and play their music at a volume causing sterility in whales out in mid-ocean.

They do things that must seem perfectly sensible to them at the time, but leave normal people shaking their heads like punch-drunk boxers. When Russ was contacted by the State Patrol, confusion was his first reaction. Seems persons in a car registered in his name were observed throwing eggs at other cars the previous Saturday night. Hmm. Matt had used the car that night because his was out of gas, but all he did was go play poker with some school friends. Under pressure he gave us this lame story that began with stopping at 7-11 to buy eggs. He said he didn't question his buddies' request to stop; probably they were going to have scrambled eggs for a midnight snack. He recited this with a trusting air, as though he actually expected us to believe him. Too bad the DUM policy didn't keep that adventure from me. I'm sure it would have bothered me a lot less at some future time.

Shawn's bedroom remodel also fell into the category of unbelievably strange behavior. Our daughter Katy's bedroom was small, so Russ enlarged it by moving a wall and including an unused stair landing. Shawn decided his room needed to be bigger, too. Since his was the largest bedroom in the house, we told him it was big enough…many times.

One afternoon we come home from work and walked into a house where a low haze of dust hung in the air, and the stair carpet was tracked with dusty footprints. We followed them and found Shawn relaxing in his room with a cold Pepsi, proudly admiring the eight-foot hole he had knocked in the wall to access the attic. "I could see this room didn't go all the way to the front of the house," he explained, "so I knew there was unused attic space there." We stood with dropped jaws until Russ shook his head sadly, then headed to Lowe's for supplies to wall in the new addition, so we wouldn't have to heat the entire attic.

The good thing about sons is that eventually they turn back into human beings. They talk in words instead of grunts and snarls. Sometimes they even let you know they don't mind being in the same family with you.

That's what occurred with my sons one summer evening when Matt was home for a visit. He'd been human again for several years, and Shawn had just recently made the transition. Out on the front porch we talked and laughed, and somehow the subject of cigars came up. My trial smoking at age sixteen lasted only three days before Mom came home early from Missionary Society and caught me frantically waving smoke out the bathroom window. There went that vice! Neither of the boys smoked, although they'd probably tried it and exercised the DUM policy. I remembered there was a stale cigar in the junk drawer, left over from when proud papas handed them out at a baby's birth. Shawn fetched it. Matt got it lit a little too expertly for my comfort level, and handed it to me. I saw stars and got dizzy. Through the ringing in my ears I could hear both sons whooping at the sight of their staid mom gasping and choking, cigar drooping from her limp hand.

It was a moment to remember. It made up for a whole slew of DUM events. They were both human again, and we enjoyed each other's company!

June, 2005

THE LURE OF THE OPEN ROAD

The whole family will be traveling to California at the end of the summer, and I've been daydreaming about how much fun it would be to rent a big RV. It would have a lot of advantages. We could play board games on the way. When we get lost, we'd all be lost at the same place, which isn't the way it usually happens.

I hear the big rigs get around ten miles to the gallon, so we'd have to take out a mortgage or sell a kidney to finance the trip. I'm kind of sad about giving up the daydream, but then I remember our previous on-the-road vacation experiences, and decide it's probably a good thing.

It's amazing, the things you call a vacation when you have four kids and not much money. My dad loaned us his pickup with a canopy for a couple of beach trips. It was wall-to-wall sleeping bags at night, so one of the older kids decided to sleep out on the ground. During the night she was visited by several of Oregon's mascot, the Slimy King-Size Slug. When she woke to a gelatinous kiss, she leaped out of the sleeping bag and into the truck in almost one smooth motion.

The next summer we took a tent to the beach with us. There were no slugs out on the sand, but the wind was so fierce we expected to see Dorothy and Toto whirl by any minute. It was like a Sahara sandstorm, only cold and wet. We ended up in the truck again, after we chased down and captured the flying tent.

Then my folks bought a little travel trailer, perfect for Oregon beach trips. The first time we used it, we were weak with hunger and halfway to California by the time we found a roadside restaurant that we could drive into and out of without backing up.

When we reached the beach campground, I got out to direct Russ backing into the campsite. We did okay for the first few feet, then he came to a stop. I figured he was probably trying to remember the directions for backing a trailer…you know, turn the wheels the opposite direction from how you really want to go. It's confusing enough to make *me* stop and think! Finally a kind man from the next campsite joined me. "Maybe you'd better let me do it, ma'am," he said politely. "Your husband's collapsed over the steering wheel, laughing."

I stomped up to the window to ask Russ what was so funny. Still wheezing and gasping, he wiped away tears of laughter and explained, "I couldn't tell if you were leading a cheer, or directing a choir. You sure weren't helping me back this thing!"

Of course, by the time we were parked and hooked up, it was raining hard. The kitchen was so tiny that everybody had to wedge into the back of the trailer while I cooked dinner. Anyone straying close was in danger of being decorated with spaghetti sauce if I turned too sharply from the stove to the table. At one point I counted noses and came up one short. Matt had taken his comic book into the tiny bathroom, with good reason. "There's too many people out there!" he shouted. He was right.

The trailer was one of those cozy vehicles where the table and benches become beds, so if one person gets sleepy, it's bedtime for everybody because you can't play Scrabble on the table, which is now their bed. The rain continued. The youngest, Shawn, was still in his bassinette, and Katy was a toddler. The two older children were smart enough to know that if this was a vacation, we'd booked the wrong cruise.

We headed home two days early, but the trip did have one beneficial effect. Without it, we probably wouldn't have been so thrilled with the trailer that my folks bought in Ocean Park. We didn't have to worry about parking it, since the wheels had been removed. When it rained, we could all be inside without getting claustrophobic. The tables didn't make into beds, so the night owls could play Scrabble while the sleepyheads slept.

Come to think of it, taking an RV to California isn't such a hot idea. The event we're attending is our son's wedding. By the time our crew arrived in Berkeley, we might be displaying some personality characteristics that I'd rather Shawn's fiancée doesn't see until the knot's tied...tied really securely!

July, 2005

GUILT TRIPS? HAH!

We were very young when our first two children were born, and after several years we decided the nest was going to be empty sooner than we'd like, and it might be a good idea to line up a couple of replacements. So we had two more.

I soon learned that the gap between the big kids and the little kids, as the pairs were quickly labeled, had used up a lot of my vitality.

With the older two, I eagerly volunteered to help on field trips, and bake goodies for PTA bake sales. With the younger two, I invented creative new ways to get out of those outings. At bake sale time, I bought Rhodes frozen bread dough and passed the results off as homemade. I bought cake donuts, slapped on frosting and sprinkles, and called it a treasured family recipe.

For the older son, I became a den mother. With the younger one, I attached Boy Scout patches to his shirt with Super Glue, and hoped it would hold up in the laundry. At birthday time, the older two took decorated homemade cupcakes to share with the class. The younger two took cupcakes homemade at a supermarket.

I should have felt guilty, but I didn't. They repaid me by ignoring guilt, themselves.

I had learned the art of laying on guilt trips at my mother's knee, and she was an old pro at the subject. With very little effort, she'd have me abjectly apologizing for even *thinking* of playing with the kids next door, instead of burnishing all the wood furniture with Olde English furniture polish, or ironing Dad's shirts. Guilt worked on our two older kids, not as effectively as Mom's had, but so-so. In the gap between the two sets of kids, I lost the knack. They shed guilt like water off a duck's back. It wasn't humanly possible to guilt them into helping by working myself into exhaustion, then collapsing over the tasty, home-cooked dinner and sighing, "I just can't do it all. If I only had some help."

When Katy and Shawn were pre-teens, I became thoroughly fed up with spending the entire weekend catching up with cleaning and chores I hadn't gotten around to after work during the week. To solve the problem I made two lists of tasks, one for the truly hateful jobs and another for the mildly obnoxious. I called a family meeting and explained the injustice of our current system (although somehow, I was the only one who considered it unjust), and assured the kids that if we all pitched in, by Saturday afternoon the work would be done and we'd all have the rest of the weekend for fun. The plan just required each person to sign up for X number of truly hateful tasks and X number of mildly obnoxious ones. I posted the list on the refrigerator door, with a pencil nearby.

The system was flawed, to say the least. Sometimes I posted the list at eight-thirty Saturday morning, and by nine o'clock it had disappeared. There were frequent accusations of one sibling putting the other one's name by the truly hated task of cleaning the bathrooms. There were obvious erasures and replacements of names on the mildly obnoxious list. Their ploy of not knowing how to do a task, resulting in Mom doing it while showing them how, didn't work even the first time. I'd used that one on my own mother, and it was good for three demonstrations before she smelled a rat.

The Saturday morning labor camp had one beneficial side effect…they got up earlier on Saturday morning, trying to be first to get to the list. After a while they wised up, rushed downstairs to make their choices, and snuck back up to bed.

One Saturday I overheard one of those conversations you'd be better off not hearing. "You know, we're going to grow up and be gone someday," Shawn said. "Who do you suppose is going to do all her work THEN? And why is she so grouchy all of a sudden?"

"Oh, it's probably that 'change' thing that women talk about all the time," Katy replied. "Metamorph, or something like that."

"I wish she'd just morph back," Shawn muttered. "This is getting real old, real quick!"

Well, kids, if I was a little bit dumber, and more nostalgic, I might apologize to you for those sweaty Saturday mornings, but I'm not. There's that old saying, "whatever doesn't kill you makes you stronger," or something to that effect. Just look how strong I helped you become. You're welcome!

September, 2005

MEMORIES OF A SPECIAL SISTER-IN-LAW

Ah, Goldendale! To our two older children, the name of that little town should have been Nirvana, or maybe Paradise. Russ's brother Don, his wife Ruth and their children lived there. Auntie Ruth was laidback and fun. She loved to have the house full of kids, and they loved being in it. My children got by there with things they never dared try at home.

Auntie Ruth and Uncle Don's son, Chuckie, was a little older than our Luanne. Their Cindy was six weeks older than our Matt. At that peaceful time, kids could wander around without being in danger. Chuck and Luanne could go fishing in a creek that was too shallow to drown in. In fact, it might have been too shallow for fish to live in, because they never caught any. Instead, they came home with coffee cans full of frogs. After hearing enough shrieks of "Get that thing away from me!" to make the effort worthwhile, they moseyed back to the creek to release them.

Cindy and Matt trailed after the two older kids, who usually tolerated them graciously, but not always. One afternoon we gave Chuck and Luanne enough money to buy four tickets to the Saturday cartoon matinee, and they headed for the theater, walking fast enough to make the two tag-alongs whine. Chuckie was a very bright little boy, with an ingenuity that sometimes made me wonder if he'd end up in the state penitentiary at Walla Walla. Luanne took equal blame for the events of that afternoon, saying the idea hadn't been just Chuckie's, but hers, too. It wasn't her usual modus operandi, so I consoled myself that she falsely 'fessed up out of loyalty to her cousin.

After the kids left, Ruth and I settled down for a peaceful chat. We were interrupted by a neighbor delivering our two younger children to the door. Seems they'd been tied to a tree a block away. They hadn't been crying…said Chuckie and Luanne were playing a new game with them, kind of like hide and seek without the seeking.

We put the two down for a nap, and waited the return of our young criminals. Eventually, we saw them trudging slowly up the street. Luanne's face was tear-stained; Chuck's extremely worried. "Where are your little brother and sister?" we asked. Luanne burst into fresh tears and Chuckie eyeballed the distance to the door. They didn't mean for anything bad to happen, they wailed. The little kids were walking so slowly they were going to make them late for the movie. Besides, they could use Cindy and Matt's ticket money for popcorn. For the rest of the visit, the two younger kids received kinder treatment from their siblings than ever before.

At Auntie Ruth's house, the usual behavior rules went out the window. It was okay to haul a can of soda all around the house, sipping and slopping. You didn't have to put a little bowl under your Popsicle, to prevent sticky drips.

Once Ruth and I made a speedy grocery store run across the street, leaving the two younger ones napping and the two older ones sedately watching TV. When we returned minutes later, we could hear the commotion from the corner. The two nappers had been awakened by the noise of the gymnastic performance in the living room, and now all four were participating. They jumped from the back of the couch to a metal TV tray, then to a hassock. The TV tray was bowed in the middle, and the one it had replaced lay in a corner with the legs hopelessly bent. For this behavior, all four were disciplined. For other, more minor events that bothered me, but not Ruth, I would make very meaningful eye contact with my two kids. My eyes said, "Boy, am I ever going to take care of this when I get you home!" They would immediately look away, pretending they hadn't seen my glare.

Ruth died of cancer three years ago, just six weeks after Don's death from the same disease. She was much too young to leave us. Cindy and her husband took loving care of both parents, and Chuck moved in to help her in the final weeks. Ruth died with grace and dignity, and near the end she assured me that if there is life after death, which she strongly believed, she would give our love to Matt.

I still have dreams about Ruth. We're in those busy, happy years. Her kids and mine are running wild, but it doesn't bother her. It's as if she's telling me, "See how they all turned out? Spilled soda and dripping Popsicles aren't the things that matter. What matters is the love."

October, 2005

FOLLOW THE LEADER…STRAIGHT INTO TROUBLE

Our parents were decent, hard-working people. My cousins and I must have been throwbacks to some shunned ancestor hidden deep in the family closet.

We were living in a cramped wartime housing project. Out on their farm, Aunt Nora was bedridden with rheumatoid arthritis and needed help. Our families had always been close, so the ideal solution was putting the two families together until Nora improved, and we found a farm of our own.

I couldn't imagine anything better than living with my two favorite cousins. Dorothy, ten years old, was cautious and sensible. The phrase I remember her saying most was some variation of, "Wait…we're gonna get in trouble…I don't think we should…" At nine, Hazel's motto was "C'mon! It'll be fun!" I was eight, easily led, too dumb to think up mischief, but eagerly going along with it. My words were "Sure!" and "Okay!" Put these three kids on a farm where the men are away working long hours, one of the mothers is bedfast and the other is eight months pregnant, and you have a recipe for disaster.

We three kids felt cheated because we didn't have a horse. Our try at catching a cow and breaking it to saddle had resulted in big trouble, but we still had the pigs. Dorothy and I sat on the metal pigsty roof and beat on it with chunks of firewood until the frenzied pigs darted out, where Hazel waited with her lasso. Then we'd have to herd them back into the sty and run the whole routine again. Hazel never did manage to lasso a pig, much less train it to be ridden, which was the next step of the plan. We were making so much noise that we didn't hear the dads drive in. Supper that night was eaten standing.

Many of our escapades started out in the spirit of helpfulness, like the lawnmower incident. In rainy southwestern Washington, you don't dawdle once the hay is ready to cut. Dad and Uncle Ted were working long hours at the shipyard, so we knew we had to help. We needed a mowing machine. That cow out in the pasture who did nothing but give milk could be more useful for a change. All we had to do was figure out how to hook her up to the push lawnmower. Unfortunately, the lawnmower hadn't yet been brought down from storage in the hayloft, and it was too heavy for us to carry down the ladder.

As we stood in the open hayloft window pondering the problem, Dorothy said, "Wait, I don't think…"

Hazel said, "Don't be such a fraidy-cat. C'mon, it'll work!"

I said, "Sure! Okay!" while Hazel pushed the lawnmower out the window. It made an impact crater and smashed into roughly a thousand pieces. Once again we had a stand-up supper.

Dorothy never weasled out of the blame, never said, "Nuh-uh, Daddy, I didn't do it. I TRIED to tell them not to." No, she just nobly zipped her lip, leaving Hazel and me filled with guilt that turned to resentment. So whenever Hazel thought of a fiendish way to get back at her, I went along. "Sure! Okay!" Sometimes the fiendish ways weren't even thought up. They just happened, like the feed barrel crisis.

One of our chores was to feed chickens and gather eggs. (Fortunately, we were unable to think of a reason to hitch a chicken to a piece of farm equipment, so the hens flourished.) Their grain was kept in a tall, skinny barrel, and we stood on an upturned milk pail to scoop it. One evening the level in the barrel was low, so Dorothy, being tallest, climbed on the bucket and leaned in. As she hung over the edge, her center of gravity unbalanced, Hazel reached out quick as lightning and gave the waving feet a little push. While Dorothy stood on her head in the barrel, her muffled shouts echoing off its sides, Hazel and I ran across the road to sneak a ride on the neighbor's recently-repaired lawn glider, declared off limits to us after we'd done a loop-the-loop in it.

Darkness fell, and Mom yoo-hooed us in to supper. Seeing the empty chair, she asked "Where's Dorothy?" Hazel and I exchanged guilty glances and jumped up. Mom followed us to the back door and heard, faint on the evening breeze, "H-e-l-p!"

The seriousness of our escapade, emphasized by the palm of Mom's hand, tamed us somewhat. You know you've been really bad when the punishment can't wait for Dad to get home.

We became less impulsive. Aunt Nora got better. Dad and Mom found a little farm we could afford. Luckily, it was two miles away from my cousins, which is probably the only reason all three of us didn't end in prison.

February, 2006

MORE THAN SWEET NOTHINGS IN THE EAR

Romance seems to be in the air on Valentine's Day, and thoughts of romance naturally lead to thoughts of marriage. Or maybe not. When compared to the long haul of marriage, romance seems as airy and insubstantial as the bubbles drifting from a child's bubble pipe on a spring day. But marriage, now…nothing airy and insubstantial there!

We celebrated our golden wedding anniversary recently, and our daughters threw a surprise party just before we left for our trip. I suspected something was up when Russ told me we should go to Portland on Saturday, even though our plane didn't take off for England until Monday morning. "But I'm getting my hair cut on Saturday afternoon," I protested. I had my lists made, I told him, and that's the biggest part of packing. What was the big rush? Finally Katy called. "Mom, I understand you don't think you need to get here Saturday afternoon. Well, you do!" So I did.

The daughters had made reservations at the Italian restaurant where Russ and I had dinner on our wedding night. We couldn't afford a honeymoon, but we could have a nice dinner at Caro Amico (which over the last fifty years has changed from a little hole in the wall place to a trendy nightspot). We entered the room and found as many of the original wedding party as they'd been able to get together on short notice. Luanne and Katy used our wedding album pictures to replicate the floral decorations. There was a beautiful cake, and the guests shared family pictures taken over the years.

Russ had spent the previous ten months gathering pictures from our photo albums, and music that was important to us, and a friend made a memorial video of them. A TV was wheeled in and as the video began, the tears soon followed. There were our parents…smiling at our wedding, then older, now gone. There WE were…young and attractive, middle-aged and a little care-worn, then old. There were our kids…babies, toddlers, school children, teenagers, adults…and one forever gone. There were the houses that had been home to us, the Christmases we had celebrated. There, in fact, was a life together.

It was lovely, but it showed only the rosy side of life. It didn't show the time five-year-old Luanne heard us arguing and went up and down the street telling the neighbors that her mama and daddy were going to get a divorce. Or the time I got mad, stormed out, drove around until I cooled off, and returned to find out he hadn't even known I was gone. There was a good football game on TV.

The memorial video didn't show the time Russ broke his wrist at his summer job, and had to depend on me for help. We had words on the first day of school, and he stomped down the sidewalk to that big important opening meeting with his shoelaces flapping in the wind, refusing to let me tie them.

Unseen were the times that in-laws seemed like outlaws except there was no price on their heads…and we might have taken care of that problem, if money hadn't been so tight.

In some of the most important times of our lives together, romance was completely nonexistent. Moonlight and roses aren't involved when you're head to head at the kitchen table, discussing teenage children and wondering why boarding schools have to be so expensive. Or when a child is seriously ill, or hurt. Or when the two of you embrace a child whose life choice means a hard road ahead. Or when you lose a child. Or when you hurt together, unable to help as you watch a grown child go through one of life's rough patches. Or when you're older, and one of you is ill, and you realize that this is the "in sickness and in health" part of those vows made so long ago…and that you wouldn't have it any other way. This person you've spent most of your life with means so much to you that you will gladly help him from bed to recliner, and make sure he remembers his medicine.

Romance is wonderful, and you don't have to be young and beautiful to enjoy it. But the long haul takes more than sweet nothings whispered in the ear. It takes something deeper, something that will last through clashes, disappointment, pain, grief, wrinkles, hair loss and hot flashes.

I'll bet you've never seen those things mentioned on a Hallmark valentine!

March, 2006

HOME PLACES

I read someplace that the average for number of houses owned in a lifetime is five. We're in our fifth house now, so I guess we'd better stop going to real estate open houses for our Sunday afternoon entertainment.

Luanne was a toddler when we bought our first little house, and Matt was born a few months later. Moving into our own home felt like reading the first few pages of a new book, knowing you're going to enjoy it right up through the "happily ever after." Russ built a sandbox in the back yard, and hung a swing from the willow tree. We suffered ear infections, tonsillectomies, and middle-of-the-night stomach flu disasters. There was always more month than there was money, but we were twenty-three and twenty-one, and the future stretched out ahead of us. How could we be anything but happy?

After a few years we decided we needed a bigger house, and bought an ugly-duckling old farmhouse in town. It towered awkwardly over the Johnny-come-lately newer homes. A friend consoled us, "Sure, it's a ranch house like all the rest. It's just standing on end, that's all." Luanne and then Matt walked to school a few blocks away, and Katy and Shawn were born while we lived there. This house saw the beginning of Camp Fire Girls, Cub Scouts, and slumber parties. With two kids and two babies, this was where I learned about multi-tasking. It was a busy, happy place.

Our next house was the one that will always be "home" in our memories. We must have had a thing for big old houses, because this one was a 1910 farmhouse in the country. It had a barn to hide in, a willow for the tree house, and a Tarzan rope swing out over the shallow irrigation ditch. The kitchen was large enough to hold seventeen people, we learned one Christmas.

This was the place where it all happened: Childhood illnesses that lasted all winter by moving at a leisurely pace from kid to kid. The year the pipes froze, and the only thing missing in our Eskimo lives was whale blubber. Fixing so many sack lunches for so many years that I could do it on automatic pilot. Those dreaded calls from the school principal. Four kids learning to drive, with the obligatory first speeding ticket and fender-bender.

But on the flip side: Snow days, Easter egg hunts, school plays, music lessons, 4-H, Christmas trees. My sewing nook on the landing at the top of the stairs, where I sipped spice tea and sewed, watching the snow drift down. Birthday parties, picnics, and sitting in the front porch swing on soft summer evenings.

The kids grew up and graduated. Luanne married out of that house. Our first grandchild was born. Matt spread his wings and moved to California, and came home to die while we lived there. Eventually, the happy memories softened even that grief. When we drive by that house now I no longer have a lump in my throat (well, just sometimes), but I'm still filled with a bittersweet nostalgia.

Our next move was a far cry from the old farmhouse…a geodesic dome perched on a hillside. It was lovely to look at, but we soon realized it wasn't a good choice for people who were no longer spring chickens. Every bag of groceries had to be hauled up a flight of stairs to the main level. On our first Christmas Eve, we dug three cars out of the snow in the steep driveway. The wall of windows gave a beautiful view, but when Russ had surgery, I was alone in an isolated house with a dog who played mind games by spending the evenings looking toward the doors and windows and growling. We lived there only two years.

Which brings us to our current house…not much larger than that first little starter. When all the kids are home for a visit, and at Christmas and Thanksgiving, we miss the big old farmhouse with its rambling space for spreading out. But the rest of the time, when it's just the cat and us, it's perfect. It's simple to clean and heat, and the yard is small enough that lawn-mowing and gardening aren't burdens, unlike the half-acre lawn out at the farmhouse.

Oh, I guess we might defy the national average and buy a sixth house, if we win the lottery. We've both always wanted a big log home. But attention, realtors: Unless you see a picture of us holding a winning lottery ticket, or a check from Ed McMahon, don't waste time on us when we visit your open house. We're just passing through!

April, 2006

MISCHIEF, MAYHEM…AND HAZEL

For a glorious eight months in my childhood, we lived with my two cousins and their parents. Dorothy, ten, was cautious and conscientious. At eight, I never thought up exciting stuff, but eagerly followed along. Nine-year-old Hazel was the life of our party. Her ideas kept us busy having fun, then trying to talk our way out of trouble.

After dropping in on a girl our age who had just moved into the neighborhood, we walked home in a dark mood. Sure, this kid was an only child, but gee whiz! She had every toy that had ever flown out of Santa's workshop. "You know, it's just not fair," Hazel said. "She's got all those dolls and ours are just junk."

"Mine's not junk," I protested.

"That's because you didn't dye her hair with food coloring, or cut her stomach open to find out what made her cry 'Ma-ma', like Hazel did," Dorothy explained. Turning to her sister, she said, "Besides, Hazel, we don't even play dolls."

"Well, that's because they're junk," Hazel declared. "If we had good ones, and all those doll clothes, we'd play with them. I have an idea." She turned around and headed back. Dorothy and I followed, even though we knew that the time span between one of Hazel's ideas and trouble was just a few hours.

Hazel explained sadly to Mrs. Frons, "We don't have any nice doll clothes, but if we could borrow these for a day, our moms could use them for patterns and sew us some." She followed this unbelievable statement with a pitiful little smile. Dorothy and I stood with open mouths. Aunt Nora's joints were so swollen with arthritis that she couldn't hold a needle. My mother not only hated sewing, but her time was completely occupied taking care of a sick woman, a toddler, and three little girls, one of whom, had her head been shaved, would probably have revealed a "666" tattooed on her scalp.

So we took the doll clothes home and played with them briefly. They were too large for my Betsy Wetsy, and looked just plain weird on Hazel's green-haired, eviscerated doll, so we stacked them up to return. "We can't take them back without washing them," Hazel said, with a dangerous gleam in her eyes.

"But they're not dirty," Dorothy protested. While I was trying to decide which cousin to follow, Hazel came through with a statement guaranteed to shut Dorothy up. "You know Mama would have a fit if we borrowed something and returned it without washing it first!"

I never quite understood how we ended up doing laundry in a mud puddle. My mother was monopolizing the sink, but that wasn't a valid excuse. I do know that my heart lurched when I first saw the red velvet fading into the white collar of the doll's coat, and that the mud edging the hem of the little embroidered dress caused an actual pain in my stomach. "They'll look better when they've dried," Hazel assured us airily, and we hung them on the barbed wire fence.

We got sidetracked nailing a ladder up the side of the cherry tree, using some mahogany planks Uncle Ted had been saving for a bookcase. Then the dads came home from work, and we experienced a thirty-minute display of Uncle Ted's tongue-tied, red-faced, vein-throbbing fury, after which we were sent to bed without supper.

Next morning we saw that the fence had left rust lines on the doll clothes that hadn't been blown off. Those didn't have rust lines, just rips from the fence barbs. We put them in a paper bag and started up the road. "You better think what to say, Hazel!" Dorothy said in an unusual display of firmness. "It was your idea!"

"All right, all right!" Hazel snapped. "I'll take care of it!" She took care of it, all right. She knocked on the door, stuck the bag in Dorothy's hands, grabbed me by the arm, and took off. We crouched behind a bush and watched. Dorothy looked after us sadly, squared her shoulders and waited for doom.

She was inside for ages. "Mrs. Frons probably called the police," Hazel said, about the time cold took the feeling from our toes. "We'd better go hide. Or maybe run away from home. We could walk out to the highway and hitchhike."

Just then Dorothy came out, pausing on the doorstep for a hug from Mrs. Frons. She still had a big smile on her face when she got to our bush. She also had hot chocolate on her breath. "Mrs. Frons said I was a brave, brave girl, with a conscience," she said proudly.

"That's what she thinks!" Hazel spat out. "She doesn't know you just can't run fast as us to get away!"

Justice was served. Dorothy enjoyed tea parties and access to a toyroom that was off limits to Hazel and me, because of our unapologetically bad behavior. However, she confessed a few months later, it hadn't been nearly as much fun as she expected. Actually, kind of boring. By that time, we were again a threesome bent on mischief and mayhem. The Frons family had moved. Something about wanting to find a neighborhood with nicer playmates for their daughter.

April, 2006

THIS IS POSITIVELY THE LAST HOUSE. I SWEAR!

I feel like such a liar. Less than two months ago I said in this column that we were living in our last house. Not wanting to sound morbid, I didn't say that I preferred being carried out in a pine box, instead of the horror of packing, holding the giant yard sale, scrubbing a house that you won't even get to enjoy being spotless, and hunting for things you're sure you packed...somewhere.

Then our daughter approached us with an interesting idea. Why not sell both our houses and buy one together? We'd afford a much nicer home than either of us own separately...some place large enough that at Christmas, the whole family could stay in one place, instead of some at our house and some at hers. She said she was pretty sure her siblings wouldn't mind. Turned out they'd discussed it when we were all together at Thanksgiving. I can just hear the conversation about what to do with Mom and Dad when they get old: "Hey, you're the one dumb enough to stay there in town like a sitting duck! You've got 'em!"

So we went house-hunting, and found one with spacious rooms, easy-to-care-for yard, and enough bedrooms to house the whole family at holidays, including her two kids who are in the bouncing age. You know, eighteen to forty, bouncing back and forth between independence and the comfort of home. The new house even has a craft room, where Luanne and I immediately saw our two sewing machines, her quilting table and my gift-wrap center.

I think the three of us will be happy housemates. There's a big family room to retreat to when we need our own space, or our taste in TV contrasts sharply. We love each other, and are considerate of each other's feelings. I actually enjoyed living in the same house when our grown kids bounced in, once I got used to the idea that they no longer had a curfew, they didn't have to eat everything on their plates, and it wasn't my duty to get them off to work on time. I learned that they'd grown into admirable human beings.

Still, there will be some problems. I'm a keeper, and she's a minimalist. She once joked (I hope) that her goal was to live so simply she could move in one afternoon with a pickup truck. Helping us haul stuff to the storage unit last week, Luanne saw a box marked "Old Magazines – New House" and moaned.

"It's not what you think," I defended. "It's just those Christmas magazines from the 60s I read every year."

Both daughters joined in helping me pack up my sewing room. We ended the job with five Hefty bags full of uncut yardage and scraps, many of them fabrics they remembered from childhood. "Look, Mom," Katy said briskly, "unless you do nothing but make patchwork quilts for a Third World country for the rest of your life, there's no way you're going to use this stuff!" I had to admit she was right. We boxed up most of the yardage for the yard sale, and gave the scraps to a church group that makes quilts for Habitat for Humanity bedrooms. The girls didn't know I'd already filled a new garbage can with the best stuff and put it in the storage unit.

Then there's the matter of décor. In this little house I aimed for English Cottage, and ended up with Cluttered Grandma: lace curtains, pouffy pillows, and walls with too many pictures because anything a kid or grandkid gave us automatically deserved wall space. My china Victorian mouse collection didn't help. Luanne loves the modern art of Kandinsky and the crisp lines of Frank Lloyd Wright. My kitchen is decorated around a print of a turn-of-the-century mother and daughter canning fruit on a big black cookstove. Luanne's is stark, clean lighthouses.

My worry about this was eased by something that happened yesterday. Russ and I were having one of those conversations that take place between people who have been together for a long, long time...the kind where we finish each other's sentences and build on each other's ideas, only to find out eventually that we're talking about two completely different subjects. I got a glimpse of Luanne watching us with a bemused expression that said, "Oh, I can hardly WAIT until we're living together."

That's when I realized this thing can work. If she can live with conversations that start with what year we bought the refrigerator now used to store Pepsi in the garage, and end with trying to remember which set of parents handed down to us the ugly brown couch of our early years, the one all the kids threw up on, then I can make some concessions, too.

I think my Carnival glass and her Kandinsky paintings will co-exist just fine!

May, 2006

ROSES AND PEONIES

Last week we drove to the cemetery outside Goldendale, as we do every Memorial Day, to put flowers on the graves of Russ's parents. It's very quiet and peaceful there, with birdsong, and the wind sighing through the pine trees and crisply flapping the flags that line the lanes, courtesy of the American Legion.

We save out some flowers from the bouquets, and after the family burial sites are decorated, we wander among the nearby graves, placing a rose here, a peony there, on the graves of family friends from Klickitat.

Klickitat was a "company town," tiny, isolated, totally dependent on the sawmill. After buying a small existing mill, the J. Neils Lumber Company brought out a core crew of workers and their families from Minnesota, where lumber was running out, to enlarge and run it. Russ's parents were one of those families, and so were the folks whose graves we visit. Away from the people and places they had known, the new Klickitat residents became an extended family. Like most families, they didn't always get along, but they were there for each other when the chips were down, in illness, hard times and death.

By the time I joined the Scofield family, that way of life was changing. The families all had cars now, and the independence they brought. Still, if you made a trip to The Dalles or Goldendale without letting people know so they could go with you, or at least send a shopping list, you had to make amends afterward.

Russ's family welcomed me in, and his mother especially enjoyed telling someone new all about Klickitat. I loved hearing it as much as she loved telling it.

I learned about dancing parties, where the men carried the furniture outside and rolled up the rugs, and the children slept on quilts behind the rugs. The parents danced to accordion, guitar or whatever live music was available, or to Victrola records. When it was almost dawn, they'd go to another house for scrambled eggs and biscuits, and then trudge home, carrying sleeping babies on their shoulders.

Grandma told me about community Christmas parties, where the company put up a big tree and Santa handed out treats. She described the Depression, when the workers' hours were cut to sometimes only a half-day a week, but the company store carried them on credit, company electricity lit their company houses, and no one went hungry or cold. She told how a hobo came through Klickitat, and the townspeople fed and warmed him, then put together a Christmas box and sent it to the family he had left in the Dust Bowl. He couldn't find work, he explained, but at least he could give them one less mouth to feed.

Their late-August camping/canning trips were an example of how women can band together and turn work into fun. The men drove the women, children and camping gear up to the huckleberry fields, and then returned to the mill to work. All week the women and kids picked berries, packed them in Mason jars, and canned them in boiling kettles over campfires. Then the men drove up and brought them home.

When a woman was sick or had a baby, other women brought their specialties. Josephine could always be counted on for her mile-high angel food cake, with hand-whipped egg whites. They pitched in, house-cleaning and child-tending, sometimes taking the older children home with them for as long as necessary.

The company put in a baseball field on the flat below the mill, and Sunday ballgames were a regular entertainment. School was the most important community function, as it still was when I came to Klickitat. Everybody attended the games and programs, whether they had a child involved or not. Grandma still drove a carload of kids to out-of-town games, even though her youngest child, Russ, was long out of school.

When boys turned sixteen, they could count on summer jobs on town-site maintenance: taking care of the ball field, painting and repairing company houses. If they were responsible enough, when they were eighteen they could work summers in the mill, which paid more. This part-time work paid for Russ's first two years of college, and allowed him to save enough to pay the hospital for our first baby, and start back to college.

Then the lumber industry dwindled. J. Neils sold the mill, and several owners later, it closed down. A small-town American way of life had ended.

Klickitat never had its own cemetery, so most of those old-timers are buried here in Goldendale, beneath the flags and pine trees. Many of those family friends (or maybe they should just be called family) are buried close by. Living near one another in life, and now lying near one another in death, they rest in this peaceful place, and we remember them with roses and peonies.

July, 2006

U-PICK? NO WAY!

We've visited a lot of Yakima Valley fruit stands over the years, putting nutritious food on the table at a cheaper price. But I've never gone the U-pick berry route. I figure I've picked enough berries in my life.

Blackberries grew viciously wild down in the Portland area where I grew up. They tried to conquer our pasture. I'd put on jeans, long sleeves and gloves, Dad would throw a ladder into the vines for us to crawl on, and we'd pick enough for jelly or a pie. The alternative to the ladder would have been a machete, and that was one of the few things he didn't have in his shop. Every couple of years Dad would splash a five-gallon can of gas on the bushes and throw in a match in a vain attempt to kill them. Next spring they'd burst into bloom even more gloriously than before.

But strawberries had to be the worst. At that time and place, country kids earned their spending money picking strawberries. Uncle Ted had a huge berry field where his daughters, (my cousins Hazel and Dorothy) and I joined neighborhood youngsters and those bussed out from town. One morning the three of us worked on adjacent rows, sprouting new crops of freckles under the blazing sun. It had rained the previous night, so our knees were caked with mud and our fingers were slimy from pulling berries out from under wet leaves. "This isn't fair!" said Hazel. She was always our ringleader, thinking up schemes that Dorothy first protested, then followed. I never wasted time protesting, just followed. "This isn't fair, because it's too hard!" Hazel continued. "I'll bet this is worse than when the slaves picked cotton." She'd learned about the Civil War in school that year. "And to think our own father is making us be slaves!"

"Daddy pays us just like the other kids, so it's not like we're slaves," Dorothy offered in her placid voice.

"Yeah, well, he's our dad and should get us everything we need without us having to work so hard for it." Hazel always had a mouth on her, but the heat had given it an edge of meanness. "I have an idea," she confided, beckoning us to her so she could demonstrate.

We watched her for a moment. Dorothy said, "I don't think that's a good idea. We're gonna get in trouble."

Hazel said, "Don't be such a scaredy-cat. We won't get caught. They won't know who picked these flats." Then, as a clincher, "We'll make twice as much money, easy. We'll make enough money to go to Jantzen Beach and eat ice cream and ride the rollercoaster and throw up."

That was enough for me. "Sure!" I agreed. So we put a light layer of strawberry leaves in the bottom of each basket, to keep the layer of dirt that we added from sifting out. Then we added about three layers of strawberries on top of the soil. The teenage boy checking in the flats and punching our picking cards complimented us on such fast picking and nice, heavy flats.

Unfortunately, we were still picking when Uncle Ted got back from his first trip to the co-op with berries. It was so hot that he'd decided not to wait until the end of the day, as he usually did. When we saw him stomping down the row toward us, Dorothy muttered, "Uh-oh." Hazel gave him a sparkling smile and said cheerily, "Hi, Daddy!"

"Don't you hi-daddy me!" Uncle Ted roared, grabbing the nearest basket and upending it. The three layers of guilt clumped there on the damp soil. I wondered briefly how he'd known we were to blame, then reminded myself that of course he knew. He'd lived with Hazel for 12 years. "My own family!" he yelled, his face crimson and a little vein in his temple pulsing. "I stood there proud as punch while they dumped out a sample. I didn't have anything to worry about. My berries are always the best. Never any green or rotten ones in Ted Hubbard's berries!" I wondered if the hot sun and rage might make his head explode. "There came the leaves and dirt. So they did another crate. Same thing. Eight bad crates! Then they dumped every dadblasted crate on the truck, to be sure!"

Uncle Ted drove me home, instead of waiting for my dad to pick me up after work. I had to explain what had happened, because I knew if I didn't, someone else would. I got one heck of a chewing-out from Dad, but I had a feeling Hazel and Dorothy got worse than that.

The next summer, though, I realized I didn't get off so easily. Dad planted his own strawberry field, and for three years I spent the first weeks of my summer vacation on my knees, filling my crates with sweat, tears and honest layers of strawberries.

That's why, when I was an adult, it wasn't U-pick, but They-pick.

September, 2006

LABOR DAY HUCKLEBERRIES

Younger daughter Katy visited over the weekend, and for Sunday breakfast she baked us a huckleberry cobbler…sort of a last hurrah before this kitchen goes Weight Watchers and pastry becomes a cardinal sin. "Where'd you get the huckleberries, Katy?" her dad asked. When she replied that she'd bought a gallon at a Highway 97 fruit stand on her last trip, he wanted to know how much she paid for them.

Her answer slowed the progress of spoons to mouths. "Maybe we'd better just gild the cobbler and use it for coffee table décor," her sister suggested. But after one taste, we knew it'd never last long enough to be a coffee table ornament. Putting it mildly, it was delicious. Wild huckleberries leave those big, wimpy, easy-to-pick domestic blueberries looking embarrassed when it comes to flavor. Sure, you run to brush your teeth after the last bite because you can practically feel the acid taking off a layer of tooth enamel, but it's worth it.

"Remember those old Labor Day huckleberry camp-outs?" Russ asked us.

Oh, my, did we remember. For years, Russ's parents and their grown kids and their families gathered at the same spot for the three-day event. A narrow lane marked the division between Yakama Reservation land and the area open to picking, and of course we were all wistfully certain that the forbidden berries just across the lane were bigger, sweeter and more abundant.

Each family had its own tent. On one trip, I had to work late and we pitched our cheap, army surplus tent in the dark. When daylight came, we awoke to laughter and jokes about whether Russ had flunked out of Boy Scouts. One look at the sagging spectacle and we had to laugh, too.

It wasn't a campground, but some kind soul in the past (LONG past) had installed a two-hole privy on our side of the lane. The kids (and some of us adults) vowed to cancel bodily functions for three days, but eventually everyone had to give in to nature.

The men dug a hole for garbage and laid a grill for cooking across the crude fire pit some past camper had made. Grandma Scofield always brought the first night's dinner from home: a big pot of More, her own invention. It got its name because eaters always held out their plates and demanded "More!" It had spaghetti or macaroni, bacon, hamburger, tomatoes, onions, green peppers, pimentos, cheese, and whatever vegetable Grandma decided to toss in. Don, Russ's brother, was the official breakfast cook because his crispy campfire fried potatoes and bacon were irresistible. Otherwise he wouldn't have been allowed to hold a cooking utensil, because he turned into a brisk, command-barking tyrant the minute he picked up a skillet. "Hand me the salt!" "What idiot put this chunk of green wood on the fire?" "What do you mean, you forgot to pack the catsup!"

After breakfast, Grandpa handed out the little metal buckets he kept stored in the attic for their once-a-year use. For a while, the air was filled with the sound of berries pinging into buckets as the cousins raced to be the first to cover the bottom of their pail with a layer of purple. Grandpa always ceremoniously awarded the winner a stick of Juicy Fruit gum. They could have the gum any time at home, of course, but it tasted better coming from Grandpa's pocket. Once the contest ended, the kids slowed down. One always spilled a pail on the ground, and in retrieving the berries, managed to scoop up a good quantity of pine needles, twigs and dirt. An older cousin scared the littler ones with tales of pickers coming face to face with a bear on the other side of the bush. Some child was always calling, "Wow, this one has a lot more berries than the rest!" followed by mass evacuation to the supposedly better picking, leaving the adults to clean half-stripped bushes.

In the evening, dinner around the campfire never tasted quite as good as Grandma's pot of More, even though appetites were fueled by fresh air, weariness and hunger. Then we heated water over the campfire for dishwashing, and saved some to get the top layer of dirt off kids at bedtime. Grandma turned back the blankets on her neat rollaway bed while we three younger women looked on jealously. She refused to sleep on the ground, and her More was so good it granted wish fulfillment. The rest of us crawled into sleeping bags, leaving our socks on so we didn't have to feel the stuff in the bottom.

"Boy, those trips were fun," somebody said as we ate our huckleberry cobbler last Sunday morning.

"Yes, they were fun," I agreed. "but you know what? I think the berries Katy bought were worth every penny!"

October, 2006

FOUR WAS REALLY ENOUGH

We had our family back in those good old days when you could have more than two children without being blamed for hogging the planet's resources. We had a girl and a boy, and then quite a few years later, another girl and boy.

The older two were excited about the younger two at first, or maybe they just put up a good front. Their enthusiasm lessened somewhat when big brother/big sister responsibility kicked in, but they were still fairly pleasant. Even when they began complaining that the little kids were getting away with things they'd never even DREAMED of trying, Luanne and Matt were never really nasty in their complaints. It probably helped that I didn't get defensive and try to deny the obvious. Yes, the two littler kids got away with more. I was older, and mellower. Also more exhausted. It was easier to ignore some things than to do something about them.

Katy and Shawn didn't mind their low-kids-on-the-totem-pole status. Big sister and brother were enough older that the two younger ones weren't even tempted to complain that they wanted equal rights and privileges. Why gripe that you don't get to stay up as late as somebody else, when you're still taking a nice long afternoon nap?

There was the slight problem of Katy wishing to be the youngest in the family, but other than out-and-out fratricide, what could she do about it? So she managed, although not always graciously.

Then when she was eight or nine, she developed this burning desire to have a baby sister. One of her classmates had a blessed event in the family, and Katy wanted one, too. I told her she already had a baby brother…Shawn. In a preview of what was to come in her teenage years, she rolled her eyes dramatically. "HIM!" she snorted. "He doesn't count. He's not a baby, and besides, he's a boy. It's a baby sister I want!"

I told her it would be snowing in He…Heaven before another baby joined this family, and considered the subject closed. Katy did not.

A few weeks later, she approached me one evening, clutching a pencil and little notebook. "I've got it all planned out here," she began earnestly. "All you have to do is *have* the baby. We'll name her Sophie." I was too stunned to interject that the people across the street had named their dog Sophie, which might prove embarrassing to her planned little sister unless the canine Sophie died young.

"That's not so bad, is it, just *having* the baby?" she continued. "I've got a schedule written down here." She showed me the little notebook. "See, I'm getting up early every morning to feed Sophie, and give her a bath and get her dressed." Katy checked the next item on her schedule. "Then I'll pack the diaper bag, put Sophie in her stroller and push her over to Mrs. Moser's house before I catch the bus. When I get home from school, I'll go get her and bring her home. Then I'll feed her, and play with her until it's time to put her to bed." Glancing up at me, she said in a matter-of-fact voice, "Her crib will be in my room, of course." She scanned the notebook page, and said, "I'll do my homework after she's gone down for the night." With a beaming, super-salesman smile she completed her pitch. "See? Not bad at all. What do you say?"

The first thing I said was "Please tell me you haven't approached Mrs. Moser with this scheme. Please!" Mrs. Moser was eighty-four…fit and active, but not quite prime babysitter age. Besides, keeping our wandering farm animals out of her imported Dutch iris garden kept her busy enough, without taking on a baby.

Then I had to break the news to Katy that poor Daddy couldn't have any more children. She was shocked, and demanded to know why. Feeling she was too young to have the word "vasectomy" in her vocabulary, I explained, "Well, the doctor just said so, that's all."

I'm glad the doctor said so. Judging by how much I gained in "mellowness" and lost in vitality between those first two sets of kids, Sophie would have been a monster. After the other kids were grown and gone she'd probably have taken control of the house. She'd have locked us in our room and piped our gruel to us through the keyhole, just letting us out long enough to use the bathroom.

I think we quit when we were ahead, with four kids!

August, 2007

GOING "BACK HOME"

Nothing illustrates that phrase "you can't go home again" as well as my annual trek into the back yard to see the much-hyped Perseids meteor shower in mid-August. I either stay up late reading or set the alarm clock to wake me in the wee small hours, wrap up in a robe for warmth and mosquito protection, and take a cup of tea outside. Leaning back in a lawn chair, I look up into the heavens and say, "Do your stuff, Perseids!"

Perseids never does its stuff. Once, out at the farm, it almost did. Maybe the sky was darker there, or maybe Perseids was just in the mood to put on a better show that year. Tired of hearing me talk every summer about how great the spectacle was going to be, Russ and the kids humored me. We set up chaise lounges and spread out sleeping bags and waited for the big event. By the time we fell asleep, one by one, we'd seen maybe twelve shooting stars.

My high expectations spoil the show for me. I keep waiting for a repeat of the Perseids meteor shower I saw in childhood, on a visit back to southern Missouri. You always remember things from childhood as bigger than they actually are…maybe that's what I'm doing with the shooting stars.

I remember lying on my back in the grass of Grandma Covey's front yard, oblivious to the bedtime chigger-check such a dumb act was causing. The day had been so hot that we'd eaten Grandma's chicken and dumplings supper out on the screened back porch, which she called her summer kitchen. Sweat had shone on all the aunts' faces when I made my half-hearted offer to dry dishes afterward. I loved suppertime at Grandma Covey's house. There were so many aunts that I could safely offer to help, secure in the knowledge that I'd be refused.

Instead of drying dishes I poked holes in the lid of a Mason jar and caught fireflies. When the aunts finished the dishes they relaxed on the veranda, and my firefly-chasing was accompanied by Aunt Laura's softly drawled, "Donna Lynne, you be careful! You fall with that jar, you'll cut yourself sure!" The uncles were in lawn chairs out in the yard, and their laughter and cigar smoke drifted to me on the tiny evening breeze that stirred the humid heat.

From the dining room window came the sound of Grandpa's radio. He never missed a baseball game or the evening news, no matter how festive the family gathering going on without him. Fortunately the town baseball team wasn't playing that night, or the lights from the field next door to Grandma and Grandpa's house would have interfered with the meteor show.

Grandpa was a great fan. Long ago he'd found a knothole in the fence and dragged out a kitchen chair, from which he watched every game. Eventually his secret got out, and the town honored him with "Arthur Covey Night," where he had a prime seat and was given recognition at the seventh-inning stretch. By the next game, he was back peering through his knothole, enjoying cheating the town out of an admission price as much as he did the game.

As I lay on my back, surrounded by the softness that I always associate with Missouri…muted laughter, breezes, drawled conversation, scent of fresh-cut grass and cigar smoke…the heavens seemed to explode with shooting stars in a huge bowl over my head. They weren't just one a minute…they were almost constant, of varying size, brightness and length of flight.

Next morning, the sound of church bells drifted in the open window as I woke. The heat upstairs had finally lessened, and as I flipped the pillow one last time to its cooler side, I remembered those beautiful shooting stars of the night before. In my child's mind, it was a Cecile B. DeMille-type epic staged only in Missouri. And maybe I was right, because I've never seen a Perseids meteor shower to compare to that one.

We had moved away when I was four, so I never really missed Missouri, although my parents always referred to it as "back home," and wanted to be buried there. A few years ago I called the flower shop in their home town to make arrangements for flowers on their grave on Memorial Day. When I gave my parents' names, they were familiar to the florist. "Why, your folks and my folks were friends," she explained in her drawl that defied locality. Maybe some people retained the manner of speaking their ancestors brought from the Deep South, like mine did. It pulled me back through time.

The voice brought me the aunts' soft laughter, fresh-cut grass against my bare feet, the uncles' muted chuckles and faint cigar smoke, Grandma's chicken and dumplings, and church bells on a Sunday morning. Most of all, it brought me a universe of shooting stars, with me at the center of that universe.

No, you can't go home again. But every August, I try one more time.

October, 2007

THE MIGHTY HUNTER

Hunting never thrilled me, but I guess I knew when I married a boy from Klickitat that it might become a part of my life. I treated it the realistic way most young brides do…ignore it and it'll surely go away. Some of his relatives affect you like fingernails on the chalkboard? Oh, why worry. What's an occasional Christmas or Thanksgiving visit? You relish sleeping in on the weekends, and he greets the sunrise with a cup of coffee? You'll meet someplace in the middle, surely. He likes ballgames, and you think they're about as exciting as watching paint dry. You like British comedy, and the scenes that make you laugh aloud don't even cause him to crack a smile. Oh, well, you'll change him.

That pretty much describes how I felt about hunting. But I was one of those '50s wives, the kind who pictured themselves raising beautiful babies in a little white cottage with roses climbing the picket fence; baking cookies, and scrubbing the wax buildup off the linoleum floor while wearing high-heels and pearls. When our husbands got home from work we were supposed to greet them with the newspaper and their slippers, and we were supposed to ENJOY THEIR INTERESTS.

Our first hunting experience came on a warm October day when we'd been married only a few weeks. Russ was hunting gray-diggers, which is like target practice, only you don't have to set the cans back up in a row after you hit them. Gray-diggers are prolific little vermin, sort of like a misbegotten cross between a rat and a chipmunk, so you have an unlimited supply of targets. I was along for the hike, and to ENJOY HIS INTEREST. On a steep hillside I'd been whining that I was stuck; I'd been able to climb up, but there was absolutely no way I could get down that cliff unless I sat and scooted all the way on my rear, which I proceeded to do. Then I heard an ominous dry rattling sound that I'd never heard before, but instantly identified. I leaped to my feet, and by the time I heard the first gunshot I was halfway down the hill. For years Russ liked to watch me shudder when he told how many rattlesnakes had been sunning themselves, and then say with a chuckle, "So you just couldn't get down that steep hillside, huh?"

Our second hunting experience (and my last) was the coldest I've ever been, other than at a couple of football games when I was in high school, but they don't count because I was having fun at the time.

We were with a group hunting deer, and Russ and I were stationed in something called a "blind." I decided that was its name because you had to be blind stupid to be there in the first place. It was a shallow hole in the ground, with a few branches thrown down to protect us from the cold earth. I think there were a couple of blankets, too, for the little good they did. We got there in what felt like the middle of the night, to wait for the deer activity that was supposed to come with daylight (remember, I'm the one who likes to sleep in on the weekend). Within minutes, I was clenching my jaws to keep my teeth from chattering, afraid the deer would hear them and be scared away. We had a thermos of coffee, and we very, very quietly poured a cup. It warmed me temporarily, and then the usual effect of coffee set in…I had to go to the bathroom, which was impossible.

I began to worry when my toes stopped hurting. By the time my fingers lost all feeling, I was wondering which of the grandmas would raise our infant daughter, and how bitter the custody battle would be. I suppose we could have cuddled for warmth, but by this time I'd sooner have cuddled with Bigfoot himself than with the hunter who'd gotten me in this mess to begin with. ENJOY HIS INTEREST, my foot! Unless his interest was hot chocolate and a roaring fire, forget it! Well after daylight we finally gave up and walked back to the car, where the rest of the group waited for us. Either they'd forgotten where we were, or there were no deer to be driven by our blind.

A couple of years later Russ finally got his deer. He figured out the cost, including the expense of all those autumns when he came home empty-handed, and came up with an astronomical per-pound figure. Factoring in the reality that although I'm a good cook, and I tried my best, I couldn't turn that venison into anything tasty, he decided to give up hunting. He confessed that he figured a Klickitat boy was supposed to enjoy it, but all he really loved was the hike.

So now he hikes without a gun, and I cook beef, not venison, and we're both happy ENJOYING OUR OWN INTERESTS!

November, 2007

LAST THINGS

We just returned from a trip to that part of Missouri that was always "back home" to my folks. I wanted to get the feel of the country again for a book I'm writing about my great-great-grandfather, told from the viewpoints of his four wives. No, he wasn't a polygamist…wives just wore out quicker back in the 1800s. And after a wife died, a man had to remarry as soon as possible, so he'd have someone to take care of the children she left behind. With a background like this, I'm not writing a heart-thumping romance, but rather a book about life in another time and place.

I'd earlier sent off for copies of land grants, and the helpful clerk at the county assessor's office marked a map for us, so we were able to stand on the very land where my ancestors built a log cabin when they came from Ohio in 1836, and the creek where my great-great-great-grandfather, Oliver, operated the first grist mill west of the Mississippi.

We plodded through wet grass and chiggers in tiny country cemeteries, deciphering the inscriptions on crumbling gravestones, and then our job was done and we headed home. I looked back at the rolling hills hazed with soft green, knowing it was the last time I would see them.

I thought about how meaningful all the last times are, even the little "last time this year" ones. The juicy, last-of-the-crop Bing cherries you buy in late July, sweet enough to leave a memory until next summer's harvest. The cold, crispy, sugary watermelon that slices in half with a good solid thunk when you cut into it in September, as a farewell to summer.

Probably my great-great-grandfather Henry shared the same feeling when he ate the last rich, custardy paw-paw fruit in October. And when the rolling Ozark foothills turned bronze and orange, he knew he'd soon see only bare branches until the next spring.

There are more important "last times," too. Walking the youngest child into the kindergarten classroom on the first day of school, realizing that this goodbye ritual will never happen again.

Attending the youngest kid's high school graduation and knowing you'll never again circle the parking lot endlessly on winter concert night, finally parking out by the football field and hiking to the auditorium. This last time event has a positive angle, though…you know that after many, many years, you've packed the last school sack lunch for them to discard, or trade for something better.

Seeing the posters come down off a bedroom wall as a kid leaves home, knowing the space is no longer "his room." But maybe this is a poor example. Our last empty bedroom was occupied sporadically for years by kids bouncing home again for short financial recuperation stays.

When he clasped a grown son's hand in parting, my great-great-grandfather would have known he was experiencing a last time. In that era going West, or even just a state or two away, required financial means and fortitude. For most people, it wasn't a round trip. Once you got there, you didn't come home again.

As she rocked a baby who slipped away with a common childhood disease, Henry's wife would have known this was the last time she'd hold the child in her arms. Those are the last times that announce themselves clearly and heart-breakingly.

Many times, though, you don't know until later that you've experienced a last-time event. It's a good thing, or you'd spend your life weighed down with apprehension.

The death of the great-great-grandfather I'm writing about illustrates the perfect "last time" event. Henry was born in 1830, and lived to be ninety-six (those four wives evidently took good care of him). According to family stories, he had been feeble for quite some time and used a cane, but one late February morning when spring was in the air, he woke up feeling wonderful. He tossed his cane aside and announced he was going to take a walk to the general store. Halfway there he dropped dead.

Talk about a perfect "last time!" I think Henry strolled along, enjoying the softened air of approaching spring after being inside all winter. He probably admired the first tiny swellings of leaves on the hickory and sycamore trees, and the gentle mounding of the Ozark foothills as they rolled to the horizon. His old eyes might have watered when he gazed up at the fluffy clouds in the blue sky, but he was cheered by the promise of spring. He was enjoying the moment, never thinking that the stroll down the country lane to the general store might be his last walk. And then he dropped dead.

Forget about rigid rituals. Hand me the sign-up sheet. I want to get my name down for a "last-time" event like Henry's!

December, 2007

A GROWNUP CHRISTMAS

Last year our daughter and grandson spent the holidays in Bolivia with granddaughter Caity. We had a wonderful Christmas with our son and daughter-in-law in Berkeley, along with younger daughter Katy and her pet, Ben the Wonder Dog. I always make home-baked dog biscuits for him, then wrap them beautifully just for the fun of watching him look guilty as he tears into the paper and ribbon. In Berkeley, Ben found one more thing to be afraid of…earthquakes.

When daughter-in-law Becky showed us around the University of California lab where she's working toward her doctorate in microbiology, I remembered the tremor of the previous night and revised my opinion about the worst place to be when the Big One comes. Maybe not the Golden Gate Bridge, after all, but in this lab surrounded by deadly bacteria and viruses in glass containers.

During our visit we had a concert of Christmas music, dinner in San Francisco's Chinatown, a boat trip and tour of Alcatraz Island, seafood on the waterfront, a barbecue on their patio, and a tour of Shawn's garage-turned-studio to see the paintings he's working on. We had a power outage during which we played Yahtzee by candlelight until we were almost blind. We had gift-opening on Christmas morning, and Becky cooked a delicious turkey dinner.

It was a wonderful grownup Christmas, and when we got back home it was to a tidy, quiet, grownup house. And I realized that what I yearned for was one of those noisy, messy, chaotic Christmases we had when the kids were growing up, out at the farm.

I wanted the traditional punch my dad always made, and proclaimed as "even better than last year." Dad grew up in the Ozarks, so I don't know where the tradition came from. I've only read about Christmas punch in books about long ago England. We had it every year, although Dad was the only one who enjoyed it. It contained chunks of fruit, and he didn't strain it, so we filtered through our teeth a mixture of thick, home-canned grape juice, cider, orange pulp, lemon seeds, spices, and whatever other juices and fruits he was inspired to use. At the end of Christmas Day I collected all the barely-touched glasses of punch hidden behind potted plants and under chairs.

I wanted to be awakened at the crack of dawn by small voices asking "Is it Christmas yet?" I wanted a Christmas morning with a lot of kids making a lot of noise, and someone mourning the gift that was water-soaked by a clumsy refill of the tree's reservoir. I even thought wistfully of the pile of torn gift wrap paper that gave a few anxious minutes listening to the roar in the chimney as you waited for a chimney fire.

I wanted to see the platters of pretty cookies I spent so much time decorating, the ones with holly and Christmas trees carved out of green gumdrops trimmed with red cinnamon candies. I even wanted to see a few of them ground into the carpet in the hubbub, as always happened. Unbelievably, I would have welcomed the sight of the dog throwing up green gumdrops in the backyard, if we were lucky enough to get him out the door in time.

I wanted to referee the annual argument between the kids about whose new board game was going to be played first. I wanted to see the unusually eager juvenile helpers rush to get the dining table cleared so we could start on the thousand-piece puzzle that would be finished by New Year's Eve, if we were lucky.

I wanted to see the kids playing with something made by my own hands…a stuffed toy, doll clothes, a tent for G.I. Joe, a personalized busy-box filled with sewing scraps and craft supplies. Never mind that I could have spent less and accomplished more at a toy store; it was those late nights in the sewing room with spicy tea and carols on the stereo that I remember.

I wanted those *Good Housekeeping* holidays where, following magazine directions, I saved the Thanksgiving turkey breast and turned it into a Santa's sleigh centerpiece for Christmas. Sure, it was ugly even after it was spray-painted red, but it was fun. And the cloud made from a round furnace filter, from which wooden bead angels with crinoline wings dangled. I had to cut into an old 1950's crinoline petticoat for the wings, and I never could get the angels balanced correctly, so the cloud hanging in the doorway was always at a slant, like a listing ship, but the kids thought it was beautiful.

Enough of wanting what I can't have! Those days are gone, and we're going to enjoy a grownup Christmas again. But the entire family is going to be here, so I'm sure I'll have all the chaos I crave. And if one of our grownup kids grinds a cookie into the carpet, I won't mind. Ben, the furry granddog, will eat it, anyhow.

Heck, I might even whip up a batch of Dad's Christmas punch!

March, 2008

HAZEL'S LEADING LITTLE ANGELS INTO TROUBLE

People who have read this column for several years are probably familiar with my cousin Hazel. Her family and mine lived together for a while during World War II. Housing was hard to find; Hazel's mom was bedfast with rheumatoid arthritis and needed help. It made sense for our two families to share a house.

I was an only child until I was seven, so living with my two cousins seemed like heaven. A year older than me, Hazel was the original wild child. If there was ever a dull or quiet moment, she was quick to come up with something to fill it…usually something that got us in trouble. Dorothy, two years older than Hazel, was slow and cautious, meek and obedient. On her own, she'd probably never have inspired even a scolding. This quality drove Hazel crazy, but she solved the problem by bulldozing Dorothy into action. As the youngest, I happily went along with whatever fun thing Hazel suggested.

It was a long walk to our country school, but Hazel quite often broke the monotony. Sometimes she'd pretend to hear a cougar scream…something that probably hadn't happened there in at least eighty years. "Listen! Didn't you hear that? There it goes again! Pull your coat collar up! They always go for the throat!" We'd arrive at home gasping after having run all the way, but got no sympathy there. "Well, if you're dumb enough to listen to Hazel, you deserve whatever you get," was my mother's response. Yes, we knew Hazel was fibbing, but she was so darned good at it that panic set in, no matter how many times she'd fooled us in the past.

Hazel was such a great pretender that she kept me believing in Santa Claus for an extra year, using the cougar technique. After we'd gone to bed on Christmas Eve, she gasped, "Listen! Don't you hear that? It's sleigh bells! It's Santa Claus! C'mon, you've GOTTA hear them! Are you deaf or something? Dorothy, you hear them, don't you?" Dorothy would answer obediently that she did indeed hear bells. Eventually, I heard the faint jingling in the distance…proof of the power of suggestion.

When I first attended the country school, I was miles behind all the students because of so many moves. Hazel was the one who stole a book from school and taught me how to read.

Poor Mrs. Bresler, with her beautiful flower garden, suffered from Hazel's leadership. We walked past it every day on the way home from school. One April day Hazel stopped and said decisively, "Our mothers should have flowers too. Ole Miz Bresler has more than she needs." Dorothy's response was the same as always: "Hazel, we're gonna get in trouble." Mine was also the same as always: "Sure! You betcha!" We picked armloads of daffodils and tulips and presented them to our mothers, but we didn't get the heartfelt gratitude Hazel had said would be ours. Instead, my mother marched us back up the road, where we had to apologize to Mrs. Bresler. Mom offered our services weeding to atone, but for some reason Mrs. Bresler didn't want us in her yard.

Hazel was the one who told us how much fun it would be to make an elaborate playhouse in the hayfield that was just ready to be cut. We didn't make the crop circles that puzzled England many years later. We made crop squares. By rolling in the grass we flattened a large room, then a hallway to another room, and another, and another. When our fathers got home from work and hooked up the mower to the tractor, thinking they'd have the job done by dark, their angry explosion told us that once again, we shouldn't have listened to Hazel. We were sent out with rakes to straighten the grass stalks upright, but it was a hopeless task. We'd done a really good job of flattening the carpet of those rooms. That cutting of hay was considerably less than it should have been.

Under Hazel's leadership we laundered the fancy doll clothes belonging to the spoiled little girl up the road. Unfortunately, we washed them in a mud puddle and hung them on a barbed wire fence to dry. It was Hazel's idea to play rodeo with the cows and pigs. Hazel pushed the lawnmower out of the hayloft and broke it into hundreds of pieces. Hazel was the source of so much fun that getting in trouble seemed a reasonable price to pay.

Hazel died last week. All those grownups who feared she'd wind up in prison were wrong. She grew up to be a perfectly respectable wife and mother of four, working in a bank until retirement…but she was still lots of fun. Then four years ago she had a stroke that left her confined to a wheelchair, with little speech ability. How awful that must have been for the hyper chatterbox that still occasionally peeked out in the mischievous grin and sparkling eyes of the respectable woman.

I can still hear Hazel's familiar words: "C'mon, it'll be fun!" I've read that Heaven is, for each person, what he or she most wants it to be. If that's true, then Hazel is on a big farm with lots of temptations, and she's leading little angels straight into trouble. But it'll be fun.

May, 2008

IT'S A BOY!

We got an interesting e-mail from our son Shawn in Berkeley last week. "We had the ultrasound this morning," it began, "and learned the sex of our baby. It's a…" followed by several blank lines, then "a…….." and more blank lines, and another "a…" And that was it! End of e-mail.

I immediately whipped off a response that had a few un-motherly bad words in it. I was not alone. It had been a group e-mail, and in one of those technical boo-boos I don't understand, some of the replies went out to everybody who had received the original e-mail. Several of Shawn and Becky's friends and relatives used unkind words similar to mine. Shawn quieted all of us with the news that their "it" is now a "he."

For a moment I thought that if there's any justice in life, this little blue bundle would be just like his father. A running, climbing ball of mischief and energy would serve Shawn right. Then I remembered what a special woman our daughter-in-law is, and how fond we are of her. Besides, that might mean their first child is their only child.

A grandson! Well, there go all those little garments trimmed with lace, ribbons and rickrack that I was going to sew. And it's a good thing common sense prevailed three years ago in that shop in Sisters, when I agonized over the hundred dollar baby dress that was a mass of lace and ruffles, with a matching shawl and photo album. (After all, if you dress a baby in something that beautiful, you need an equally special book to put the pictures in.) At the time I didn't even have prospects of another grandchild, much less knowledge of its gender, so finally I walked out the shop door, feeling deprived but virtuous.

Hmmm. A little grandson. Now I feel better about the book I sent Shawn a few weeks ago. I sewed Becky a couple of maternity tops, and sent the book with them. "I Can't Wait to Meet My Daddy," it's called. It's beautiful and meaningful, but seemed a little slanted to a tossing-a-ball-out-in-the-backyard relationship. Now that slant is okay.

Having one of each, I know grandsons are as enjoyable as granddaughters. I thought back on the fun that grandson Steve and I shared…the Halloween costumes, story-time marathons, craft projects, sock puppets, watching cartoons together. He was my Nickelodeon buddy until, unlike his grandma, he outgrew the Rugrats. Unfortunately, I never did. I remembered the time we got so carried away decorating Easter eggs that we stopped twice to boil more and went through six dozen before exhaustion ended the effort. I recalled watching him proudly tooling up and down the driveway in his battery-powered Jeep.

He even provided entertainment for his great-grandmother. After he'd spent some time with my mom in her apartment up the street from our house, he told me he and Grandma Hubbard had been playing cars. Unable to wrap my mind around the concept, I asked for details. Using the layout of village streets I'd found at the fabric store and his Matchbox vehicles, they did indeed play cars…Steve on his hands and knees, and Grandma Hubbard moving hers with her cane. Great-grandchildren brightened Mom's last years.

Ah, those were the good old grandmothering days. And now I get a chance for a re-run. Better yet, I don't even need ribbons, rickrack and lace. I remember all those overalls and sun-suits I made when Steve was a baby. There were miniature "muscle pants," tiny boxer shorts for summer, and hooded fleece sweatshirts for winter. Why, there was even a dressy outfit of pants and vest, with matching shirt, for Easter one year. And all those genderless things I can sew… a hooded wrap-around towel for bath time, stuffed toys, activity books. Oh, I'll have fun!

Yesterday I bought a piece of fabric; pale blue seersucker with a pattern of little cars and trains. When I showed it to my husband, he touched it and said, "Isn't that kind of a crisp texture for a tiny baby's skin?"

"Oh, it'll be soft after I pre-wash it," I explained. "Besides, it's not for a TINY baby. It's a sun-suit for the next summer, when he's a year old."

Russ just shook his head. Grandpas evidently don't dream as far ahead as grandmas do.

I was afraid that since our grandkids aren't children anymore…they're twenty-six and twenty-one…I might have forgotten how to be a grandma. But I don't think that's a problem. It's all coming back to me now. I'm remembering the way a toddler's eyes light up when he spots grandma; the feel of a butterfly kiss on the chin because the little one can't reach any higher; that soft, warm weight against your breast when a baby falls asleep in your arms.

I can hardly wait!

September, 2008

AUTUMN...BITTERSWEET

Autumn is my favorite time of year. On a chilly morning the flannel robe comes from the back of the closet, and I slip on the fuzzy slippers that haven't been worn since May. In the balmy afternoon the windows can be thrown open. The chilly evening reminds me that soon it'll be time to get out the crockpot and perfume the house with simmering beef stew.

Every fall I read Washington Irving's "Legend of Sleepy Hollow," not for the scary Headless Horseman part, but for the glowing description of autumn country life in the Catskills two hundred years ago.

I pull open the cupboard doors in the sewing room to survey the fabric stash, and began planning Christmas projects. It matters little that for the last eight or ten years I've sworn there'd be no more Christmas projects. Autumn destroys my vow of abstinence.

Sometimes we squeeze in a last-of-the-season picnic up one of the mountain passes, combining the panorama of trees changing color with roasting hotdogs over a welcome fire. We always forget that autumn yellow jackets are even meaner than summer yellow jackets. And they love hotdogs.

As I look back on my childhood Septembers and Octobers, they're hazed with gold, like maple leaves. I know that has to be faulty memory, because the Portland/Vancouver area has more days of gray gloom than gold glory. Still, what I remember is walking through our little orchard and plucking a warm apple for an after-school snack...riding on top of a load of hay from the field to the barn, surrounded by a haze of sun shining through chaff...gathering nuts from under the filbert trees, and spreading them on newspapers until they're dry enough to slip from their husks.

When our children were all at home, autumn meant changing gears. The lazy summer was over. No more staying up late and sleeping in next morning. No more impromptu picnics or snatch-from-the-pantry, heat-it-up-yourself suppers. No more ragged cut-offs and faded tee-shirts. Back to alarm clocks, schedules, after-school activities, evening events. Back to weekly menu posted on the refrigerator, first person home put it in the oven. Back to homework and assembly line lunch packing.

Although autumn meant a faster pace, I still loved it. There's something about the season that nourishes nostalgia, even in a busy person. Events of just a few years ago become worthy of reminiscence.

Then we lost our oldest son one autumn. He came home at summer's end and died in late September. The next year, and for many years, that wonderful blend of balmy days with crisp mornings and evenings brought memories of a different kind. I saw the little boy starting off to his first day of school. I saw him practicing and falling with his first bike, climbing back on and trying it again until he got it right. I saw him busy and happy in high school, and getting his first job. I saw him spreading his wings and flying off on his own, full of the confidence of untried youth.

And then I relived the afternoon I drove down our long driveway after work and saw Matt wrapped in a patchwork quilt, sitting in the porch swing on the veranda of our old farmhouse. It was a beautiful day, he said. It made him want to get a bike out of the garage and go for a ride. But he didn't have the strength for it, so he wrapped himself in a quilt to stay warm, and enjoyed autumn from the porch swing.

Although my mind still refused to accept it, something deep inside me knew that no matter how I fought the knowledge, the doctor was right. On that amber afternoon, I realized for the first time that we were going to lose our son.

For a long time autumn was, for me, a time to shut out the beauty, lower my head and forge on, to keep desperately busy until the change of season brought a measure of relief.

Gradually, autumn became golden again. It's a bittersweet season now, because of course the old memories don't disappear. They just get farther away, and distance blurs them enough to dull the sharp edges of pain.

Now I love the season once again. I know that's what Matt would have wanted, because he loved life. He savored the crockpot beef stew, and battling yellow jackets for a hotdog. He loved the changing seasons, and the now-forbidden scent of burning leaves. He seized the enjoyment of life. When he could no longer seize it, he wrapped himself in a quilt and let it seep into his spirit.

How could I not love it?

November, 2008

NEW GRANDBABY – OLD ROCKING CHAIR

We made an eventful trip to Berkeley in September, and saw two important things...a very new grandson and a very old rocking chair.

First, the grandson. Shawn and Becky's baby son was born in mid-August, and named Jasper Denny Scofield (Denny is his Grandpa Scofield's middle name). We received e-mailed pictures of him regularly, the first taken when he was just a few hours old. We saw him turn from a blanket-wrapped little bundle to an infant with a budding personality.

Just before we left for Berkeley we received a picture of a kid with an attitude. When we made a trip through Montana during the summer, I'd told Jasper's mommy and daddy that I'd tried to find him a little cowboy outfit, since that's cowboy country. I knew the idea was sort of tasteless, I told them, so they were probably lucky I hadn't succeeded. To show me that Jasper was indeed cowboy material, they snapped a picture of him at one month old, dressed in a tiny western shirt and mini-cowboy hat (one-pint, not ten-gallon). The expression on the baby's face was priceless. It said, "What the heck do you guys think you're doing? I didn't sign on for this kind of embarrassment!"

That attitude reminded me a lot of another little boy I'd known...his daddy. I couldn't wait to see Jasper in the flesh.

On the trip down, the closer we got to Berkeley, the more my excitement grew. Remember that fizzy sensation you felt as a child, waking early on Christmas morning and knowing you couldn't get out of bed until daylight? Well, that was the feeling I had...simmering, restless anticipation.

I was brought down a few degrees when we almost hit a deer with a death-wish in southern Oregon, but it didn't take long to bounce back up. We reached Berkeley, and thought briefly that it might be nice to not show up until Shawn got home from work, so he could give us the first showing. Nah, I decided. Dumb idea. I couldn't wait that long.

Jasper is even more adorable than I'd expected...no biased grandma opinion here, of course. We took enough pictures that the Jasper screensaver slide show on my computer lasts for about ten minutes. Productivity is slowed down when I watch the whole show before I begin writing. I look very strange in many of the pictures where I'm holding him. My mouth is in weird shapes and my forehead is creased. That's because I was singing to him, and your mouth always looks funny on vowels. The forehead creases came from deep thought. I was having a hard time remembering the words to a lullaby not sung for twenty years. I know it started with "Go to sleepy, little baby," and ended with "Ride a shiny little pony," but what came in the middle?

In some of the pictures the little boy with an attitude peeks out. He's looking at me with an expression that says, "Who let this strange woman in? You've got to be more careful about keeping the doors locked!"

Yes, that attitude took me back many years, but the other important thing we saw, the old rocking chair, took me farther.

That rocking chair was the first piece of furniture we bought. It came from a second-hand store down by the harbor in Bellingham. Luckily it cost only $2.50, because we couldn't afford much more, and we needed it to rock our infant daughter.

It rocked all four of our children. I rested my tired body in it for many middle-of-the-night feedings. The babies grew, and the chair matured with them. It was perfect for soothing toddlers with earaches.

Eventually the kids didn't need to be rocked, and the chair moved out to the veranda. It was the ideal place to enjoy the music of frogs and Rainbird sprinklers on soft summer evenings.

The grandkids came along, and our daughter hauled the rocker to her house. Being bashed by Tonka trucks and exposed to weather on the veranda had left it in need of a facelift, so she sanded off the scars and refinished it. The chair spent some fruitful years rocking babies again.

In retirement, it suffered the indignity of being the "extra chair," brought out only when there were more people than places to put them.

Last year I made it a seat cushion, back pad and matching footstool in Christmas fabric, and it enjoyed the holiday with the family again.

When Shawn and Becky were here for our granddaughter's wedding in June, they took the rocking chair back with them. It was time for it to return to duty.

Now it's a satiny light moss green, the perfect contrast for Shawn's vivid paintings on the walls. No pastel lambs for baby Jasper. Secure in Mommy or Daddy's arms, his eyes lock onto the bright primary colors and slashing lines of the pictures.

Maybe in future years the old rocker will be a delicate pink, or its original golden oak. But for right now, moss green is just right. And I think it's happy to welcome baby Jasper, and to be restored to active service after years of idleness.

Just like me!

January, 2009

FLORENCE NIGHTINGALE? NOT!

I observed New Year's Eve in a different way this year…sitting by my husband's hospital bedside holding the little barf basin, waiting for him to throw up. Anesthesia does bad things to his touchy stomach.

Russ had a hip revision on New Year's Eve morning, replacing the artificial hip joint he received twenty years ago, at a relatively young age. "Play sports, exercise, take care of your body, and what good does it do you?" I asked him then. "Your body just falls apart sooner." I didn't say anything smart-alecky this time, since I'm beginning to experience some of the things your treacherous body does as you get older. However, after learning from Russ's doctor the candid details of what the surgery would entail, I decided that any of MY aching body parts are staying firmly attached. My mother didn't raise any idiots, but she did raise a lily-livered coward.

We prepared well for the hospitalization and recuperation. When I did my Christmas shopping I got a few books he's been wanting to read, and then had to keep him out of bookstores so he wouldn't buy them himself. The kids and grandkids got him things to break the monotony, and the wireless internet hookup our daughter received for Christmas will benefit him, too. He can surf the net from bed, or from the straight chair he'll occupy for a while. His cushy, comfy recliner is forbidden during healing.

He opened two gifts that gave me a horrifying glimpse into the future: tabletop bowling, and a "Learn to Play the Harmonica" kit. I can just see myself crawling around on the floor retrieving little bowling pins and balls that rolled off the table, while he accompanies me with the blow out, suck in "whoo-whah" of a beginning harmoniac…er, beginning musician. Guiltily I remembered the year my dad gave one of our toddlers a harmonica for Christmas. I managed to accidentally step on it really hard by New Year's Eve.

The surgery went well, and then came the barfing-in-the-basin part. Even horrible things come to an end (although at the time, Russ didn't appreciate my Pollyanna comment) and eventually the barfing stopped. Then came pain and boredom.

Medication took care of the pain part, and our daughter had left the cribbage board and cards, which we hoped would help with the boredom problem. When you combine Russ's level of sedation, and the fact that we hadn't played cribbage for at least thirty years, you have a unique game of cribbage. We made four starts, stopping each time because we'd done something stupid, or couldn't remember what to do next. A nurse asked who was winning, and I replied, "Umm…nobody." Russ just moaned softly. The constant shuffling of cards kept him occupied, though.

I went home and found our Hoyle's rule book for games, with its yellowed, dog-eared pages and torn cover. It was first copyrighted in 1887, and ours was the 1948 reprinting, but I guess cribbage rules don't change much in a century. Just leafing through the book was a nostalgia trip. It belonged to Russ's parents, and has hand-written instructions for games somebody played years ago, like Liverpool Rummy.

Russ is home now, and I'm learning how to be a kind, gentle caregiver, even though there are times it goes against my true disposition. Getting the therapeutic support hose on him should be easy, since his legs are so skinny. But it's like trying to cram a queen-size leg into petite-size pantyhose. There I was trying to be gentle while working out the wrinkles, with him twisting and jerking because his feet are so ticklish.

A little while ago I helped him from his straight chair back into bed, fixed his lunch of choice, served it on a bed-tray, fluffed his pillows, brought fresh water and gave him a pain pill. He said something as I turned to leave. I didn't quite catch his words, so I responded, "Have a nice sleep," and wondered why he burst into laughter. Turns out his gratitude had prompted him to say "I love you," and my response hadn't been quite what he expected.

Ah, well, we'll make it okay. Unless he starts playing table-top bowling and learning the harmonica. If that happens, I'll bring out the pain medication and the cribbage board. I'll either give him a pill or just whap him upside the head with the cribbage board. Whichever works best. But it'll be a kind, gentle whap.

February, 2009

CALENDAR STRESS

I just served Russ his lunch of roast beef with gravy, mashed potatoes and mixed vegetables, with grape juice to drink. He looked down at the tray in confusion. He'd ordered ham and swiss on rye (heavy on the Gulden's Brown Mustard) with ginger ale to drink.

He raised his head and said sadly, "I guess this means the recuperation honeymoon is over."

"It's good!" I said in a sweetly impatient voice. "It's not just a TV dinner, it's a Marie Callender Slow-Roasted Beef Homestyle Meal! And we're out of ginger ale." Then, feeling a little guilty, I threw him a bone. "Your fruit jello is jelling even as we speak. And not with just fruit cocktail. With marshmallows and bananas and extra maraschino cherries…lots of them." He looked a little happier. Our kids always thought jello was too much like fruit to be considered a true dessert, but Russ loves it. "And don't forget that homemade tapioca last week," I added.

That was a special request. Not just tapioca, but tapioca cream, with the meringue folded in. I'd started with a recuperation supply of the handy little pudding cups from the grocery store, but when he said with a sigh, "Boy, some of that fancy tapioca you used to make would sure taste good," I got out the double-boiler for the pudding and the electric mixer for the meringue.

"A bowl of the yummy jello will show you the recuperation honeymoon isn't over," I told him. "Now eat your Slow-Roasted Beef Homestyle Meal."

Truth of the matter was that I'd found the TV dinner while hanging over the edge of the freezer for 15 minutes, looking for the four chicken breasts that had to be in there somewhere. Marie Callender was on the bottom, under last summer's popsicles, and I figured her homemade goodness was probably on its last legs. Ham and swiss on rye could wait for another day.

I never found the chicken breasts, and I really needed them. My hairdresser friend had just called and said, "You owe me a chicken! You were supposed to be here at 12:30." A quick check showed I'd written "haircut - 12:30" on my calendar. However, I'd written "2:15" on my brain. Last time I made such a big boo-boo I brought her a deli roast chicken. I figured this time I had to do better…like my special chicken tortilla casserole. Hence the search for chicken breasts.

I'm either terminally flaky, getting senile, or suffering calendar stress. I prefer to blame the latter. For too long we've had a lazy retirement schedule of doing what we want, when we want, and now there are all these little things to remember: Medicine schedule, home health nurse and physical therapist visits, lab tests, checking to see if Russ has done his prescribed exercises. Actually, that last one is unnecessary. He's always already done the exercises when I ask him, and is recovering from his hip replacement very rapidly. But it's fun to nag Mr. Physical Fitness about the importance of exercise.

The only other time I was this flaky was when our younger daughter, Katy, was born. It'd been quite a few years since I'd had a tiny baby around. Combining the infant timelines like how long between feedings, how many minutes to boil the bottles in the sterilizer, well-baby exams and when to give the vitamin drops, with the bigger-kid schedules of swimming lessons, dental appointments and birthday parties, put me into overload. Suddenly I was melting out the bottoms of sterilizer pans and filling the house with the reek of burning rubber nipples. I dropped kids off for appointments and forgot to pick them up. Previously, I'd shopped for a birthday party gift with the invitee, spent time to get just the right gift, and wrapped it beautifully. Now I was swinging into the drugstore on the way to the party, buying the first thing that looked halfway suitable and cramming it into a purchased gift bag, and adding a generic birthday card. Since I was in a huge rush and often chose the card by the picture on the front, the kid was just lucky it didn't say "Get well soon!" or "Congratulations on your new baby!"

I recovered back then, and turned into the normal, well-organized person I had previously been. I can do it again. Soon all the little jottings on the calendar will dwindle away. And the weather will get nicer, so I can take us for a relaxing car ride. Russ enjoyed the drive last night to a restaurant, where we had Chinese food with the rest of the family. "Mama, look at the lights!" he crowed. "Wow, cars going fast! Whee!"

I guess if he can top his pain and inconvenience off with laughter, I certainly should be able to spoil him a little longer. What the heck…I think I'll go in the kitchen and make another batch of tapioca cream!

April, 2009

SWIMMING LIKE A ROCK

I've decided to learn to swim. I waited a long time to make this step, but my reasoning is sound. It's not that I expect to fall off a cruise ship and have to dog-paddle to the lifesaver ring. Nor do I plan on leaping into a river to save my floundering child…they all know how to swim. It's just that I decided it'd be nice to have some form of exercise I actually enjoy. Something that doesn't make me happy to get sick, because it means I can avoid the machines at the gym with a clear conscience.

My good friend is a dedicated lifelong swimmer and also an excellent swimming instructor. (I consider a good friend to be someone who knows your weaknesses and likes you anyhow.) She readily agreed to give me lessons, so we signed up at the pool.

My water exercise classes, which I actually enjoy, have gone a long way toward removing my fear of water. I no longer start to panic and hyperventilate when the water reaches my chest. I can even get my head completely under water and raise it in a dignified fashion, without leaping up gasping and spluttering.

The lessons went well at first. I learned to stick my face in the water and blow bubbles, just like my kids did when they were little, while I sat on the grass at Franklin Park and watched them protectively. Then it was time to float on my back. For some reason this wasn't too hard for me. First my friend supported my shoulders, then my head. Soon all it took for confidence was just one finger under my head, and then I was able to back-float on my own, and even make the necessary frog-like movements to propel myself along.

This had been fairly painless, so I was eager to get to the next step: floating on my stomach. When my friend was halfway down the pool with the other student, I decided to try it on my own. I launched myself face-first into the water, and simultaneously into panic mode. I'd figured it would be a simple matter to just stand up. Wrong. The most charitable description of my actions would be "helplessly flailing." I lurched ever forward. Occasionally a toe touched the bottom, then I floundered forward again. At first I was thinking,

"Oh, I hope nobody sees this humiliating spectacle." This was immediately followed by, "I'm going to drown! I'm going to drown in the shallow end of the pool!" The only correct thing I remembered was not to breathe in. When once in a while my head broke the surface I grabbed a mouthful of air. Along toward the last it was part air, and the rest water.

I reached the side of the pool about the same time my friend got to me. "What happened?" she demanded.

"I was…cough, splutter…learning to….gag, gasp…float on my stomach." I replied, when I got enough breath to speak.

"Never try new things by yourself," my friend said tersely. I could see she was rethinking this "knowing the weaknesses and liking the person anyhow" part of friendship.

So we started the INSTRUCTED face-down floating, where I could regain the confidence shattered by my do-it-yourself impulse. Or so we thought. I was supposed to take a deep breath, stretch my arms forward, blow my breath out slowly under water, and float to the surface. I was only to reach for her hands when it was absolutely necessary. Turns out it was absolutely necessary as soon as my face touched the water. I've never gotten to the float-to-the -surface part.

With visualization, meditation, and very stern self-scolding, I've come to a record of maybe two seconds before reaching for her hands. And it's a more dignified reaching now, not grabbing in panic…well, maybe just a little panic. My instructor's not going to give up, because it would spoil her forty-plus year record of teaching people to swim. I tell her it wouldn't really ruin her record; nobody else can teach a rock to float, either.

I suppose I could be satisfied to just swim on my back, but there are so many drawbacks. My face would be sunburned, while the rest of me was winter white. My swimsuit would be faded on the stomach and bright blue on the back. And you can't see where you're going when you're floating on your back. I'd be bashing my head into the walls of the pool, or into little children who were out there swimming like dolphins.

So I'm going to try again. It hasn't turned into fun yet, but I keep telling myself it will. And even if it's just a teensy bit of fun, it'll be more enjoyable than those machines!

May, 2009

A VISIT FROM MY GRANDMA

The mailman delivered me a wonderful surprise yesterday from the widower of Hazel, that wicked cousin who led me into trouble (but always fun) in my childhood. After my aunt and uncle died, Hazel and her husband moved into the house where she'd grown up. She's gone now, and he's sorting and disposing of not only the possessions of their 50-plus years of marriage, but of Hazel's childhood as well.

The surprise was a book of bible stories for children, and written on the inside cover were the words, "To Donna Lynne, from Grandma and Grandpa." I think it must have arrived during the time we lived with Hazel's family, and was overlooked when we moved to our own home. The book itself wasn't familiar to me, probably because we couldn't spare much time for bible stories when it came. We were too busy staging pig rodeos, trying to harness the milk cow to pull the hay-wagon, and getting into countless other escapades, always led by Hazel, who homed in on trouble like a heat-seeking missile.

Although I didn't remember the book, oh, what a pleasure to see Grandma Hubbard's familiar handwriting again. It brought her back to me.

My two grandmothers were very different. My mom was the oldest of nine children, and her mother wasn't too thrilled with the whole kid scene, although I did have a few good years with her before all my little cousins began arriving.

But with my other grandmother, my dad's mom, it was a different relationship, Grandma Hubbard and I had a special connection. She read to me, sang with me, nurtured me. I was four years old when we moved out to California, and how I missed her.

One day the mailman brought me a package from Grandma. Inside was a doll and a complete wardrobe. I recognized scraps from clothing Grandma had sewed for me in the doll's wardrobe, and they made it all the more precious. I smoothed the dresses, nighties, coat and bonnet with my fingertips, picked up the doll, and said, "Oh, it's Nancy Light!"

I have no idea where the name came from, but I still remember the complete lack of surprise at the gift, even though it wasn't my birthday or Christmas. After all, the gift came from Grandma, and that was what Grandma was like. She knew I missed her, and needed cheering up. So she stitched her heart into Nancy Light's clothing, and sent her to me.

A few years ago we visited the area in Missouri where my dad had grown up, and where I'd visited Grandma again at the age of five, a year after our move to California. The little Ozark foothills community of Cedar Springs was gone, abandoned by residents moving to town, and then flattened by a twister 20-some years ago. But I knew Grandma's house hadn't been far away, so we drove country lanes, looking for it.

As the road wound up the hill it narrowed and the homes were far apart. Suddenly I cried, "Stop!" I stared at a small, rundown house badly in need of paint. The building looked familiar, but it was its placement, and the yard behind it, that convinced me. Too ragged and rugged to be called a lawn, it worked its way up a steep hillside. Over sixty years ago I had played in that yard. There was the stump where I arranged pieces of broken china for my dolls' dishes. There was the backdoor where Grandma had handed me bread, butter and sugar sandwiches, cut into tiny pieces to share with my doll. This little house from long ago was the place I'd been looking for.

Now, as I hold the bible story book in my hands, I'm filled with memories like the ones I experienced when we found Grandma's house that day ... memories of her deep, husky voice when she played the guitar and sang ballads I've never heard elsewhere, that must have come with her people from North Carolina. The warmth of her lap when she told me stories. The unique smell of the cupboard she called her pie safe...spices, flour, fruit...when she opened it to take out the treats she had ready when we visited as I grew older, after they had moved to town. We came back only every four years or so, and how she must have planned for those times. While we were there Dad always had his favorites: potato cakes, salmon croquettes, macaroni and cheese, stewed tomatoes with dumplings, dried peach pie...cheap, tasty foods that he remembered her cooking during the Depression, when he was young. In my mind I see her busy hands sewing, quilting, and crafting paper flowers. I remember the activities her creative mind dreamed up for me.

I'm sending a thank-you letter to Hazel's widower today. He probably thought it was just a book he wrapped and mailed. But it was more. He sent me a visit with Grandma.

June 2009

JUST LET ME BE A WORKER BEE, PLEASE!

I recently read an inspirational magazine article about women bettering the world with their work as volunteer leaders. It reminded me of my own efforts. In fact, it reminded me so strongly that I snorted "Hah!" and threw the magazine across the room. Then I brewed myself a cup of tea and found a good mystery to read.

My heart was in the right place when I volunteered, and I think I probably made a few lives better, one-on-one. Just leave me out of leadership. Let me labor back behind the front lines. W-a-a-y back.

The Chicken Tamale Stew incident is a good example. The church group needed to make money, and selling lunch at a bazaar seemed like a painless way to do it. I'd used Russ's mother's recipe for the stew often for my family. It has a cornmeal base, with chunks of chicken, tomatoes, corn, green chiles and just the right spicy seasonings. It's delicious.

I volunteered the recipe, and my dubious leadership skill. It was a smashing success. I was kept busy afterward jotting down the recipe for folks who asked. We fed many, many people who went away happy. Unfortunately, after expenses, we cleared $8.37. I don't know if we served too generously, or I made a mistake in calculating what the supplies would cost…math was never my strong suit. I was never again asked to be in charge of a church fundraiser.

As one of the worker bees, I did fine. At bake sales my homemade bread was usually the first to be sold out. If you wrap the loaf while it's still warm enough to create a little bit of steam on the plastic wrap, homemade bread is hard to resist. Some folks might raise their eyebrows when I use the term "homemade," but I say it's silly to split hairs. After all, those loaves of Rhodes frozen bread dough spent some time in my oven before they went to the bake sale. Doesn't that qualify as homemade?

If I'd been in CHARGE of a bake sale, however, it probably would have featured the best cook bringing five custard pies, and being closed down by the health department.

The Christmas advent calendars were another example of a great idea falling off the rails.

The AIDS support group we were involved in needed money for the good things we wanted to do. I wrote a children's Christmas story about a family of loveable mice who lived under the kitchen floor of an old farmhouse. It had 24 short chapters, one to be read aloud every evening from December 1 to Christmas Eve.

We made calendars of red felt, with 24 pockets sewn on each. Then we gathered up cute Christmas designs from coloring books, and traced them on felt to trim the calendars. We all had fun on the project, being more artistic then we'd ever have expected. Sure, one of the guys got a bit too anatomically correct when making Scottie puppies, but I was able to neuter 23 of the little critters with quick snips of my sewing scissors.

All our meetings became work sessions. I got tired of hauling all that stuff in and out of my sewing room, so I just left it in the backseat. From September through November, my car looked like a traveling yard sale. Or maybe a car on its way to the landfill.

At last all the calendars were trimmed. We spent a couple of meetings rolling each chapter like a little scroll, tying it with red ribbon and putting it in the proper pocket. Then, after finding a few calendars with chapters in wrong pockets, we spent another meeting double-checking each one.

Ah, the big day! Bazaar season arrived! We sold seven calendars…not even enough to reimburse me for the felt. Once again, I was removed from a group's A-list of fundraisers…probably down to the Z-list. I was back to visiting people in the hospital, driving sick people to medical appointments, and cooking homemade dishes to tempt picky appetites.

All us old-timers of that first support group meet every summer for a potluck supper. We renew friendships from years ago, sometimes shed a tear for the loss of someone we loved and helped, and talk over old experiences. They're kind when chatting about my advent calendar project; just say what fun it was, and nothing about the fact that it was a disastrous failure. We're all pretty mellow by the time the subject comes up, anyhow. We've either had, or are about to have, a dish of Florence's peach cobbler, the reason we keep coming back each summer. The crust is so light that if it didn't have a dollop of whipped cream on top of it, it'd float up into the clouds.

I'm grateful for that dessert. I'd much rather have everybody go home remembering Florence LeMaster's peach cobbler than Donna Scofield's advent calendars!

October, 2009

MAN'S BEST FRIEND?

Everybody knows how valuable service dogs are to disabled people. Why, we're learning now that they even raise spirits and calm stress in people who are dreadfully ill.

I think all dogs are service animals, in one way or another. The other day we witnessed this in action. The dog was obviously a physical trainer for people who want to become long-distance runners.

A family pulled into a park on Lake Pend Orielle, where we were admiring the scenery. The instant the passenger door opened their dog leaped out and made a mad dash for freedom. Dad, having evidently witnessed this event a few too many times, gave a disgusted look at the fleeing dog and headed for the lake. Mom and the three kids sprang into action. All of them whistled and called, while the long, lean pre-teen girl who must have been the designated chaser took off in pursuit.

I think we'll see this person in the summer Olympics some year. Her arms pumped like pistons and her strides ate up the distance, but the dog stayed ahead all the way up to the highway. Just as we were ready to drive a little farther up the road and head him off, the girl gave a giant, desperate leap and caught him. Her endurance training was finished for the day. She probably panted until suppertime.

Our older daughter's dog Snickers, who has now gone to the Great Doggy Daycare in the Sky, used to wait by the front door for somebody to not close it quickly enough when they came in or out. Once out the door he immediately became deaf to calls and whistles, trotting jauntily up one side and down the other of their block. His service ability was in patience training. He came home when he was darned good and ready, and yipped to be let in.

Ben, our younger daughter's dog, participates in the same area of service. He never leaves the yard, though. When she starts loading her car for the trip home, he frolics playfully, crouching and wagging his tail until she's almost close enough to grab his collar, then bouncing away. Even that old standby trick, rattling kibble in a metal dish, doesn't lure him in. But when she starts the car he runs over and hops in, afraid she's leaving without him.

Our granddaughter's dog, Zeus, is part Corgi and part some mystery breed whose genes were never meant to mingle with a Corgi's. But Zeus has the Corgi herding instinct. He wants all his people in the same room. He gets very stressed when we babysit him because I'm a night person. Every 20 minutes from 11:00 p.m. until 2:00 a.m., my usual bedtime, he leaves his bed and pads down the hallway to gaze fixedly at me for a while, clearly thinking "What is WRONG with this woman?"

We all know that since man first tamed him, the dog's main service duty has been as a watchdog and protector. Out at the farm, our Skipper behaved as though he'd read the property deed. When we let him out each morning he traveled the borders and then came home to breakfast. One morning he didn't come back. Neighbors had warned us about a pack of dogs that had been menacing livestock, so Russ went searching for Skipper. He found him, bleeding and mauled, in the pasture, where he had evidently protected our cows from the pack. The vet stitched him up and he came through okay, although the indignity of being carried out for toilet duty seemed to humiliate him.

When we lived in the geodesic dome, isolated and with the entire living room consisting of walls of windows, our dog was great security for me. She was fine when Russ was home, but when he was out of town, she patrolled from window to window and door to door, growling menacingly at the darkness. Soon the hair on the back of my neck was raised almost as much as on hers, and I was imagining sounds that didn't exist and building booby-traps that would clatter to the floor if a door was forced. All the times I yelled "shush!" at her probably harmed her service instinct.

Our two daughters' dogs surely had their protective instinct harmed on one camping trip. The two women and two grandkids were tucked snugly into their sleeping bags and the dogs, Ben and Snickers, were at their secondary duty of keeping sleepers' feet warm when they began to bark and growl. The women spent 15 minutes scolding "Hush!", "Be quiet!", and "It's just a chipmunk, you idiot!"

Next morning when they unzipped the tent door, they were missing a cooler, camp stove, gas lantern and portable radio. Luckily the dogs couldn't sneer scornfully, but I'll bet they were thinking, "Hah! Just a chipmunk, my foot!"

On the other hand, they probably stepped temporarily into another service role. I'm sure their owners needed their spirits raised and their stress calmed.

November, 2009

MOVE OVER, MARTHA STEWART!

This time every year I get a warm inner flush (no, not hot flashes, much nicer that that). It happens when I look out the window and see threatening gray skies, and birds gathering around the feeder in the backyard like folks at the free sample stands at Costco. It helps if a strong wind comes up and whines around the eaves, and carries the tired autumn leaves to a new resting place. . .preferably in some else's yard.

The holidays are coming! I buy the November issues of women's magazines, even though I know they'll just contain warmed-up versions of ideas and recipes that have been around for years.

I drag out all my holiday help books from the basement for a new search. Who knows, maybe the *Gooseberry Patch* Thanksgiving recipes that I've given a thumbs-down for the last ten years might rate a thumbs-up this year. Maybe I'll try that spiced cranberry aspic chilled in scooped-out oranges shells, instead of dumping Ocean Spray canned sauce in a fancy dish and stirring it with a fork so it loses the shape of the can. Maybe the family will make Brussels sprouts a holiday tradition once they've tasted them with bourbon and pecans, instead of passing them down the table, calling them "mutant dwarf cabbages."

Appetizers? Yes, why not. Crab-stuffed mushrooms, maybe, or that recipe for smoked salmon tartlets. Of course, any kind of appetizer will seem exotic to people who usually only have slivers of turkey snatched when my back is turned, and olives filched from the relish tray.

Dessert? Every year it's same-old, same-old. But pumpkin pie won't make an appearance this holiday season. I'm thinking crème brulee, and I'll use the tiny confectionery blowtorch to caramelize the topping right at the table. It'll be like that cherry flambé I tried once, only this time I'll be sure to take the batteries out of the smoke alarm first.

Yes sir, this will be a Martha Stewart Thanksgiving. The football game on TV will be turned OFF, not just down. There will be soft and soothing chamber music instead, a fine background for the cultured conversation around the table.

I think I'll make place cards. Maybe I could glue on gilded acorns, if I can find the acorns and learn how to gild them.

There has to be a centerpiece. A roast turkey in the middle of the table is not a centerpiece, no matter how beautiful it is. It's just tacky. Handy, but tacky. I need to buy Martha Stewart's magazine. It'll have lots of home decorating ideas for the holiday. None of those trashy things like crocheting a toilet paper cover in autumn colors, but good stuff like making a wreath trimmed with oak leaves, garnished with gilded acorns (depending on my success with the place cards, of course).

Ooh, these magazines have wonderful after-dinner ideas, too. None of that loosening the belt and sitting around burping while watching football for the men, or piling dirty pans in the sink and collapsing from exhaustion for the women. We'll have games, but not the same old ones we play every year. Here's a wonderful idea for charades. I'll have to get started finding the props, of course. That's what makes the game better than ordinary…a box of original props. Let's see, I'll need a tiara, a toy microphone, a large world globe…

But it'll be worth the trouble. It'll give the game back the class it lost last time we played, when I had to make them guess Michael Jackson. I held up my arm and pulled on the imaginary trademark single glove, and they guessed I was picking cherries. I thought briefly about gliding across the floor in that moonwalk thing Jackson did, but I was afraid of falling and breaking a hip. So I used the only thing left I remembered about Michael Jackson. They caught right on when I grabbed my crotch.

Oh, are we ever going to build some traditions this Thanksgiving! Here's a great one from my *McCall's* November, 1972 magazine: Knit matching mittens for everyone in the family. Set a pair by each person's plate and place their silverware inside. After dinner, the entire family puts on their new mittens, and they all join hands and go for a walk, serenading the neighborhood with an early caroling party. Somebody carries a big thermos jug of hot cider, for refreshment along the way.

Okay, maybe that's one tradition we won't build. First of all, I'd have to learn how to knit, and there's not a ghost of a chance that will happen. Second, I can't imagine all of us in the mood for a brisk walk at the same time, and some of us will be so tired we can hardly stand, much less walk. Third, there'd have to be something a lot stronger than hot cider in that thermos jug to get us singing carols to the neighbors on Thanksgiving evening.

But I'm not through yet. I'm going to get started on my projects before the holiday flush dies down and I return to normal. Move over, Martha!

December, 2009

SONGS OF CHRISTMASES PAST

I guess it's time to put the Christmas music away for another year. You can only stay wrapped in nostalgia for so long, and then it's time to move on.

When I listen to Christmas music, I remember. It stirs the senses like certain smells or tastes, and brings the past back clearly.

Music was an important part of my growing up. Dad came from a musical family, so we sang together for fun on many dreary winter Saturday evenings. At Christmas time, carols floated from the radio all day. When I hear the music now, I remember those childhood Christmases.

"O Holy Night" brings back my ninth Christmas, when I was hospitalized with pneumonia. There must have been a lot of illness that winter. The hospital was so overcrowded that my bed was out in the hallway. That suited me fine, because the Christmas tree wasn't far from the foot of my bed. The first thing I saw each time I opened my eyes was the glow of the fancy, newly-invented bubble lights. I was so close to the lobby that the music drifted to me, and although I wasn't familiar with "O Holy Night," I immediately loved it.

The hospital priest stopped to visit me. Evidently feeling sorry for this skinny little kid in the hospital at Christmastime, he asked if I'd enjoy some comic books, then left to find some. A while later he returned, and sheepishly said, "I couldn't find any comics, but maybe you'd enjoy this. You can keep it," and handed me a copy of Dickens' "A Christmas Carol."

I'd learned to read late, because we'd moved so many times. When we finally settled in one place, my cousins taught me how to read so I wouldn't humiliate them at our little country school. Now I opened the book and was captivated by that sentence. "Marley was dead, to begin with," sent chills down my spine.

A nurse came with needle poised for my penicillin shot and saw what I was reading. "That book's too old for you," she scolded. "Father John doesn't know much about what children like. Let's give that one back to him and I'll see what I can find."

But I wouldn't trade. I read while I drank my broth and ate my red Jello. When lights-out time came, I explained that I wasn't sleepy at all and was allowed to read on. It was well after midnight when Tiny Tim said, "God bless us, everyone," and I turned out my light.

The doctor released me on Christmas Eve morning. Mom made a bed for me on the couch, so I could be a part of Christmas. Dad fixed me some of his hot lemonade, which he said could cure anything but dandruff. Christmas carols flowed from the radio, and good smells drifted from the kitchen, where Mom was doing baking that she hadn't had the heart for while I was in the hospital. Rain lashed against the windows and wind howled around the eaves, but I felt warm and secure and full of Christmas. That feeling returns when I hear "O Holy Night."

"Away in a Manger" was probably with me all my life, but the first time I distinctly remember it was when I was about seven, and sang it with my Sunday school class. We attended a little country church where each year, the children performed the Nativity story for the grownups. In our bed sheet gowns and tinsel halos, we sang the song, tripped on the sheets, replaced the slipping halos, and managed to knock down a plywood lamb on the way to our seats.

Afterward, we joined our parents and sang more songs, but none compared to our performance of "Away in a Manger." Then Santa came (evidently there were no qualms about mixing religion and a folk festival) and handed out little brown paper bags at the door as we left. The treat was always the same, but that didn't stop us from being thrilled when we peeked in at the orange, nuts and hard candy.

When I hear "Away in a Manger" I can still smell that combination of wet wool coats, Christmas tree, and oranges.

"Here Comes Santa Claus" brings back the shopping trip with Mom and Dad when I was ten years old. Dad worked nights, so I got to miss a day of school, my little sister and brother were left with a neighbor, and just the three of us went Christmas shopping. We had club sandwiches and Cokes at the dime-store counter (an unheard-of treat) and chose carefully (and frugally) for everyone on the list.

The trip became even more special on Christmas morning, when Dad gave me the music box I'd longingly admired at Woolworth's.

The weather that day was unusually clear and cold for Vancouver. "Here Comes Santa Claus" jingled through the crisp air from the loudspeaker, and when I hear it now, I remember that special day with my mother and father.

As I listen to music and the Ghost of Christmas Past comes to call, I re-live those warm Christmases. I hope my own children will someday hear a song that brings a sweet memory from childhood. It has to be one of the best gifts a parent can give.

January, 2010

A MONKEY CHAIR FOR THE LITTLE MONKEY

Although I had vowed to stay out of the sewing room this year, I made grandson Jasper an armchair for Christmas. I've never been good about sticking to sensible resolutions. It only took the better part of three days. The fabric and stuffing cost just slightly less than the kid-size La-Z-Boy recliner we saw at Costco (after I'd already bought all the supplies).

First I sewed the slipcover, a knock-your-socks-off green fleece with a pattern of monkeys munching bananas, perfectly matching the monkey pajamas I made, and the slippers from Old Navy. It was a breeze. I studied it for a while and told myself that as long as it was shaped like an armchair, why couldn't I just skip the part about making pillow forms and fastening them together with Velcro. I'd just stuff the slipcover!

The finished project reminded me a lot of old age. Everything went south, and I ended up with a big fat bottom and not much up top. The under part of the arms hung down flabbily, reminding me of why I no longer wear sleeveless blouses.

So I pulled out the mountain of stuffing, leaving the sewing room looking like Antarctica on a windy day. Then I cut out the pillow forms the pattern instructed, reread the directions six or seven times, and wrapped gifts for the next two days. I told myself there was no rush. As long as I had the project finished for our after-Christmas visit in Berkeley with Jasper (oh, and his parents, of course), everything would be fine.

The day after Christmas I sewed the pillow forms, ironed on the Velcro, and stuffed them with that white mountain of fluff that by this time had drifted to every flat surface in the sewing room. I tried to attach the pillow forms to each other and found that the Velcro pieces weren't aligned, so they didn't match up.

I pulled out all the stuffing, re-aligned the strips, and stuffed them AGAIN. That's when I discovered I'd used Velcro that isn't strong enough to hold tightly stuffed pillows together.

I fought off the urge to throw a lighted match into the sewing room. Instead I gently shut the door and started a game of Scrabble on the computer. When our older daughter saw me there, she said, "Isn't technology wonderful? Whoever would have thought you could make an armchair while sitting at the computer!"

Our younger daughter was a little kinder. "Why don't you just put all the pieces in a big trash bag and drop it off at Good Will?" she suggested.

Everybody except the Berkeley part of the family was home for the holiday, and the armchair was the focus of interest. Anybody who came in after a trip to the festive, unencumbered-by-armchair outside world asked "How's Grandma doing with the armchair?" or "Is Mom hysterical yet?" They asked each other, not me, since I had access to dangerous weapons like sharp scissors and darning needles.

I ripped off all the Velcro and sewed the stuffed pieces together with a darning needle and heavy buttonhole thread. It took a long, long time, but fortunately the slipcover hides the bloodstains made by darning needle jabs. Then I pulled the monkey slipcover over the pillow forms and sewed everything together at the bottom. Voila! An armchair! I put it in the middle of the kitchen table, with a candle on either side, and hauled anybody who dropped by in to see it.The chair rode to Berkeley in the backseat. I covered it with a blanket anytime we left the car, so some bedazzled onlooker wouldn't break in to steal it.

Jasper was napping when we arrived, and when he woke he ran to the chair and plopped himself down in it, like a young king on his throne.

Seeing this little grandson in action is a déjà vu experience. Just like his father did, Jasper begins ramping up the energy level about half an hour before bedtime. One of his favorite activities at this time was running across the room and throwing himself into his monkey chair, either bottom-first or head-first. Sometimes he'd relax, rest his head on the soft fleece arm and close his eyes. Then an adult says, "Oh, Jasper's getting sleepy." At this, with his eyes still tightly closed, he smiles an impish little grin and shakes his head so hard in denial that it seems his brains would be scrambled.

It was a wonderful visit. Jasper is entranced by trains, so we had a ride on a steam train. At story time we routinely spent twenty minutes on the train page of his Richard Scarry picture book. He cooked for us in the kitchen Santa brought him, stirring the pretend oatmeal and pouring the pretend coffee. We visited a toy store (BOY, did we visit a toy store!) and when he saw a little rolling pin he grabbed it and began rolling out pretend dough. (Yes, of course we bought the rolling pin…among other things.)

It was dismal and foggy when we left, which matched my spirits perfectly. Russ said I was entitled to tears when I cried for a little while. Home again, we loaded pictures from the camera onto the computer and admired the little monkey in the monkey chair.

Now I wish I hadn't wadded up the pattern pieces and thrown them in the fireplace. I'll want to make Jasper another one when the buttonhole thread wears out and all the stuffing heads south!

May, 2010

THE HAPPY SOUNDS HOME

We had a fun visit in Seattle two months ago with 18-month-old grandson Jasper and his mom. Our daughter-in-law, Becky, flew up from Berkeley with him for a job interview. We rented a room within walking distance of the site and they spent the night with us there, so he could get re-acquainted before the interview next morning.

Knowing he might have forgotten us since the last visit, I brought a few new toys to soften the blow when Becky walked out the hotel room door. I saved the biggest one for that actual event, but couldn't resist hauling one out right away. He knew immediately what the Fisher-Price Sesame Street toy laptop computer was for, since he sees his mommy using her own laptop often. He even "helped" me on mine on our last visit, and combined key-strokes for some strange results that I haven't been able to duplicate.

I saved the Fisher-Price camera for dinnertime. I well remembered restaurant visits when Jasper's daddy was his age. They were contests to see if we could finish the meal by the time Shawn's hunger was satisfied, because once that happened, it was downhill all the way. We knew we had to be at the exit before he progressed to bellows of rage. The mischievous glint in Jasper's eye reminds me very much of his daddy.

In Seattle, there was a nice seafood restaurant within walking distance, so with Jasper in his stroller, we three adults sauntered down for dinner. Service was slow, and I pulled the Fisher-Price camera out of my Grandma/Mary Poppins bag. I'm sure the patrons around us thought our table was occupied by a goofy family, because we all took turns posing as Jasper snapped our photographs. And of course he enjoyed picture-taking more if we made crazy faces for the camera. Grandpa won the most belly-laughs.

Back at the hotel, we had the special treat of a butterfly kiss goodnight from Jasper before he went down for the night in the Pack 'n Play we'd borrowed from Vicki, our across-the-street neighbor.

Next morning, Jasper got a little apprehensive when he saw his mommy in her dress-for-success interview suit. As she was ready to leave, I pulled out the big guns…the Fisher Price Happy Sounds Home. It was in a Christmas bag, the only container I'd been able to find that was large enough to keep it hidden until the right moment, and I'd stashed it in the closet.

I put the brightly-colored bag on the end of a bed and it pulled Jasper like a magnet. He couldn't reach it. He isn't talking much yet, but I could easily translate what he jabbered in his language: "Give me that bag, Grandma! I know bags with Santa Claus on them have good stuff in them. Give it to me NOW and nobody gets hurt!"

When I didn't obey he grabbed his mother by the finger and pulled her to the bag, where he pointed at it and tattled on me for not giving it to him in the first place. Becky told him calmly, "Grandma will get it for you in a minute. Bye-bye," kissed him and eased out the door.

As the door clicked shut and he looked at it with alarm, I put the bag on the floor and pulled out the Happy Sounds Home, with its round Little People family, and Jasper forgot the closing door. We made the dryer buzz to show the laundry was ready to take out. We rang the phone and the round mom hurried to the kitchen to answer it. We ding-donged the doorbell and let the round dad take care of opening the door. Grandpa was the Happy Sounds champion because his plots involved slapstick.

The best sound of all was the whoosh of the flushing toilet. Anybody who has spent time around toddlers knows the fascination that sound holds for them. They enjoy it most when a toy or daddy's sock is being sent to clog the plumbing, but they like it even when nothing but water swirls down the pipe. Maybe it's because the handle is just the right height for them to reach, and they experience the power of causing noise and creating the fascinating whirlpool. Whatever the reason, the toilet lid in that Happy Sounds Home was put down countless times, since that's what triggers the whoosh. This might truly be an educational toy. Maybe Jasper will be the first male who doesn't have to be specially taught to put the seat down!

Fortunately, Becky didn't have room in her luggage to take the house back to Berkeley. There'll probably be more Seattle interviews before she gets the research job that will let them move up here. I figure the Happy Sounds Home toilet flush will cover the click of the door as his mother leaves very nicely!

May, 2010

REMBRANDT WE'RE NOT!

It took many months, but my husband finally got up enough nerve to try painting again after the paint-on-the-carpet incident, when the corner of the brick hearth and a patch of carpet became pale green as he painted a living room wall.

This time he'd only done a small square on the bathroom wall when he called, "Oh-oh, you'd better come see this. It looks pink to me."

I hurried in. It did look pink. It was supposed to be peach, the exact color of the inside of the seashells in the pictures hanging on the wall, and in the shower and window curtains. I squinted my eyes and tried imagining it on all the walls. Oh, come on! Surely it was peach. The word was even in its name.

Sounding more assured than I felt, I said, "It's perfect. It's exactly right." Russ still looked skeptical, so I said, "You've got a problem with pink. Remember that bathroom out at the farm?"

We were planning a trip to my folks' place at Long Beach. Russ loved the beach about as much as I loved camping…not much…but he was going along for the sake of the family. Then he had a brilliant idea. If I took the kids by myself and let him stay home, he'd paint that bathroom I'd been whining about for months while we were gone. It didn't take me long to decide. He wasn't much fun at the beach anyhow, getting annoyed because of the sand between his toes, and griping about having to build a driftwood windbreak to keep from freezing to death in the middle of summer.

We finished loading the car and he got ready to go out to Sears and get the paint. Pale pink, I reminded him. Very pale pink.

When we got back from the beach I hurried to see the pale pink bathroom. Even from the end of the hallway, it glowed like a lantern. I gave a little shriek. "That's not pale pink!"

"Well, it's pink," Russ argued. "It's got pink in the name. Carnival Pink. It was on sale." We lived with garish Carnival Pink for three years. I never again let him pick out paint by himself, but I'll have to admit I wasn't always a success at paint-picking myself.

We had ample opportunity for decorating in the 1910 farmhouse. When we moved in, the dining end of the big living-dining room was papered with an English hunting scene in dark browns and greens. The only brightness was that rascally fox they were chasing. And since a roofed veranda ran around the front and side of the house, not much light came in the windows. We had to do something to lighten the room.

As soon as we could afford the project, we began peeling off wallpaper, and learned that a house built in 1910 has many layers to peel. The history of the house was revealed in layers…frothy ferns, trailing ivy, Chinese fans, paisley feathers. Finally we got down to the cabbage roses that adorned the room in the beginning, and replaced it with a tasteful light beige tweed-looking print. It was only our second experience with wallpaper hanging, but this time we were smart enough to choose a design where you didn't have to match the pattern at seams. You could even hang a piece upside down and not tell the difference. It went so well we decided to do the front hallway in the same paper.

Unfortunately, the front hallway was open to the second story ceiling. Using a combination of ladders and planks propped on stair rails and sawhorses, we were lucky neither of us ended up in the emergency room. We had our share of excitement, though, with me holding Russ's legs while he teetered on the stair rail. I learned what it feels like to have a moist, freshly pasted sheet of wallpaper fall on your head, paste side down. But finally we finished, and eventually realized that now the living room had to lose its dull green walls. And we knew we definitely weren't going to wallpaper it.

I chose Taco Tan, my paint boo-boo that matched Russ's Carnival Pink. It was described as "warm golden sun shining on desert sand." The sample looked very appealing, and able to brighten a dark room. When that sample appeared on all the walls, it was less pleasing. The kids were old enough by now to be mouthy, since we did our redecorating over the years, as we could afford it and had time to do it. One said it wasn't Taco Tan, it was Baby Poop Yellow. I figured she hadn't changed enough diapers to be an expert on the color of baby poop, so I ignored the comment. Another said it was the color of Halloween pumpkins at Christmas, or maybe Valentine's Day. He had a point.

Now, years later, I remembered Carnival Pink and crossed my fingers. Superstition must work. When finished, the bathroom was exactly the peach shade of the inside of a seashell. We've redeemed ourselves for the Carnival Pink and Taco Tan of long ago.

May, 2010

BEWARE: TODDLER IN TRANSIT

Whoopie! Our Berkeley family is moving up to Seattle. Now we won't have to get re-acquainted with our little grandson Jasper each time we see him!

Russ and I are flying down to help them with the move. He'll ride north with son Shawn in the rental van, and I'll ride with daughter-in-law Becky, to help her with Jasper.

We won't try to stay together. We tried that once before. The result was getting separated, with one party saying, "Oh, what the heck!" and whizzing through to L.A., while the other party said, "Oh, maybe they've had a terrible accident," and stopped at seven Highway Patrol offices to frantically check on them. Shawn and his father were in the "Oh, what the heck" truck. Our older daughter and I were in the "Oh, maybe they've had a terrible accident" car. When we finally reconnected in L.A., there wasn't much conversation for awhile.

On this trip, the two parties will have completely different goals. Shawn's and Russ's plan is to be able to turn the rental van in as soon as possible, to save money. They'll probably stop only to gas up, snatch a quick meal, and visit a rest stop when Mother Nature says it's absolutely necessary.

Becky's and my goal is to drive from Berkeley, California to Seattle, Washington, without the spontaneous combustion of a twenty-two-month-old little boy. We'll be spending the night at a motel for a good night's sleep, and stopping at parks to let him run off steam when we sense that he's nearing the explosive stage.

I remember a trip with our older daughter when she was about Jasper's age. Russ had classes, so I took advantage of a long weekend to drive to Ridgefield with Luanne to visit my parents. This was in that dangerous age before child safety seats, so Russ installed the special backseat safety door locks, and we put boxes on the floor between the front and back seats to make a level surface, then covered the whole area with soft quilts and blankets. We piled pillows around all the sides and loaded in Luanne's favorite toys, and I had a box of kiddy-type snacks and a thermos of juice within my reach.

We surveyed our work and pronounced it perfect. Any child would be happy to ride there.

During the entire distance between Bellingham and Ridgefield, Washington, Luanne ignored her luxurious play area. She stood on the soft quilts directly behind me and picked at a mole on my neck. Once at Ridgefield, we had a pleasant visit. I had the mole removed immediately after the trip.

I also remembered a family I observed at a rest stop one night a few years back. The parents had made a comfy bed in the rear of their station wagon, with pillows, games and stuffed toys. Mom had changed him into pajamas and they were trying to get him back in the car. She was peeling his fingers from where they gripped the car door-jamb in desperate resistance while he sobbed and whined, "I changed my mind. I don't WANNA go to Grandma's house!"

Since we're flying down, I can't take the Fisher Price Happy Sounds Home that kept Jasper pleasantly occupied both times we stayed with him in Seattle while his mom had job interviews. But I'm sure Becky will load the car with a good supply of toys, snacks and water. I'll have room in my bag to tuck in the fabric Goldilocks and the Three Bears house that I finally ordered on the internet, after realizing that I'd probably never finish the one I started twenty-six years ago for our first grandchild.

Then I remembered the Quiet Book. I made one many years ago for our younger daughter and son. It was perfect. I made another one years later for our oldest grandchild. It was pretty good. I'm almost finished with the one I'm making for Jasper, and it's going to be…so-so. I keep turning back to the first pages I made and realizing I should replace them. The pony whose tail can be snapped off and on isn't exactly centered on the page. The tepee that unzips to reveal a picture of him is supposed to teach a kid how to zip. Unfortunately, the zipper is tough even for me, much less a not-quite-two-year-old. The felt flowers that are supposed to button onto the stems, to teach a child how to button, ended up too thick and hard to make buttonholes in. The directions said to glue two layers of felt together to make the flowers tough and durable. I think the craft glue I bought could probably hold airplane parts together in a flight over the Atlantic. My sewing machine needle definitely isn't a match for it. So I'll have to use Velcro, and my success rate with Velcro is ultra-dubious, judging by the trouble I had with it when I made Jasper's chair for Christmas.

Oh, well, it's the thought that counts, right? My backup plan involves watching Fisher-Price DVDs with Jasper on Becky's laptop. Maybe if Grandma adds narration, it won't really be baby-sitting by TV.

July, 2010

WHEW…A FEW FINISHED SEWING PROJECTS!

Finally I can stop kicking myself for buying all that Brambly Hedge fabric on e-Bay years ago!

Maybe you're not familiar with Brambly Hedge. It's author/artist Jill Barklem's creation about families of field mice who live in England's woods and hedgerows…sort of like Beatrix Potter's drawings, but incredibly detailed. Then, around 20 years ago, an enterprising fabric designer created ten or so Brambly Hedge cotton prints, now discontinued and unavailable.

I thought I'd make quilts for future grandchildren, although at that time more grandchildren weren't even a twinkle in anybody's eye. By the time another grandchild came along, vivid colors and modern designs were what nurseries were all about. Babies wouldn't be interested in little English mice who store their food in tree trunk pantries, cook in fireplace kettles and go to holiday parties dressed in Victorian garb. But GRANDMA was still interested. Every so often I'd admire the fabric again, sigh and stash it back on its sewing room shelf.

Then our older daughter Luanne took up quilting, joined a club and progressed to designing her own projects. A few weeks ago she offered to make a Brambly Hedge comforter…not crib size, but queen size. After all, the room that has all the Brambly Hedge framed posters and glassware should have a comforter to match.

I'd thought of it myself, but am honest enough to know that my expertise ends with crib quilts with random designs, where you can whack off edges to keep them square. Besides, I have a tendency to procrastinate, and I don't have unlimited years left. I really didn't like the vision of a half-finished Brambly Hedge shroud at my viewing. But Luanne had designed a beautiful wedding quilt for her daughter and got it completed before their second anniversary. That beat my record of dangling projects six ways to sundown.

So she laid out all those fabrics with delicate pastel backgrounds. The little mice had different activities in each print, but the overall theme blended them nicely. She assigned me the job of appliquéing some of the smaller scenes onto larger solid squares. Naively I asked if I should sew them on in straight, even patterns, or scatter them randomly. It didn't hurt my feelings when she advised random. "That way it won't matter when they're crooked," she said. It was obvious that she's seen my previous attempts at appliqué.

I kept getting sidetracked admiring Wilfred Woodmouse, who leads his friend Primrose into adventures. Then I'd try identifying all the tiny items in the Storehouse Stump, and the sewing machine would limp to a stop.

But I finally finished the appliqué, and assigned myself a new task. I'm going through all the scraps and saving anything bigger than three inches square. I figure if I sew them all together in a patchwork pattern, there'll be enough fabric to make curtains to match the coverlet. And maybe pillow shams.

This creative rush is inspiring me to new heights. I think I'll dig deep and find that cloth Goldilocks and the Three Bears House I started for granddaughter Caity when she was two years old, and finish it. Right now it consists of two walls sewed to a floor, but when it's completed it'll have doors and windows that open, soft-stuffed beds, chairs and tables, and little stuffed Goldilocks, Papa, Mama and Baby Bear. New grandson Jasper, just a toddler, will love it. And granddaughter Caity won't mind that she didn't get it, since she's now twenty-eight years old.

Then I might see if I can find that Winnie the Pooh group pattern. I made Winnie and then swore off the project, but I'm pretty sure I didn't throw the pattern in the fireplace, much as I was tempted. The older kids loved Winnie. Young Jasper would enjoy Roo and Piglet, maybe even Tigger, depending on how long my patience holds out.

And I can get an early start on Christmas with the holiday fabric I've accumulated over the years. When I purged the sewing room contents prior to moving to this house, I hid that particular stash and smuggled it in. I mean, you can't throw away Christmas! Now I'll sew together all those cloth books, tree ornaments and advent calendars. I might even tackle the complicated patchwork baskets, the ones that gave me a fierce headache just reading the directions. Why, I'll have such a stock I could even hold my own bazaar!

But in the meantime I've got to cut out and sew all these little scraps together, being careful not to lop off any of the vital parts, like

Wilfred's head or Primrose's basket. When I work with the square about Dusty and Daisy Dogwood's wedding, I've got to be sure I don't stitch over the top tier of the wedding cake, or the flower tiara holding Daisy's veil. It's intricate stuff, this patchwork.

To be honest, I probably won't get to all those unfinished projects. I'll end up with a valance, not curtains. And my Brambly Hedge pillows might be pincushions, instead. But at least all that e-Bay material isn't going to waste!

July, 2010

WHERE THERE'S A WILL, THERE'S A WAY

We just finished a depressing task…making wills.

After all the t's were crossed and i's dotted, signatures witnessed and notary seals stamped, there was one thing left. Fill out this form about who gets what personal possessions, we were advised. Not really a legal document, but saves hard feelings when you're gone.

At first I was resistant, but then I remembered how my maternal grandmother verbally promised her glassware collection to all her daughters and daughters-in-law, causing some to not speak to each other for the rest of their lives.

A more recent ugly memory presented itself…someone at the viewing reaching into the coffin and removing a cheap but sentimentally valued ring that had been verbally promised to someone else. The someone else had decided that if Grandma loved the ring that much, she should be buried with it on her finger. My poor husband shuttled between the two parties, pouring oil on troubled waters. His efforts resulted in the whole family being able to sit in the same row at the funeral.

So the next time all the kids are home, we'll hand out sheets on which they're to list what they want. A friend warned me that I might get my feelings hurt if I share her experience, and find that nobody wants anything. Hopefully all our material possessions will be old and worthless by the time we check out, but there might be some things that inspire sentimental childhood memories. I hope.

Then I thought of the family pictures. In my grandma's case, one angry relative took them all, and refused to share. Her daughter still has them, and is following her mother's tradition. This is the same branch of the family that razor-bladed those important sheets listing births, marriages and deaths out of the old Bible, then sadistically gave the book to the relative working on genealogy, who had been asking for it. I know our kids would never behave like my vindictive aunts, but in this age of technology there's no reason to have to share pictures.

So I started a project that I'll probably still be working on when the Grim Reaper rings the doorbell. I'm scanning fifty years of family photo albums into the computer and making disks for each of the kids. And there are more than albums…there's the cardboard box full of snapshots, and collage frames lining both sides of the hallway. The scanner will probably have to be replaced midway through the project, but that's a small price to pay for history.

Of course I won't be doing this alone. Russ will be prying rubber-cemented photos out of collage frames and putting them back in the right places after I've copied them. Same with all those albums I started out so neatly, with kids' names, ages and description of the event written below the pictures. Then onto the later albums, when every couple of years I'd take a shoebox full of snapshots and fill some albums, hoping the pictures were in chronological order, guessing at the age of the child and groping to remember the event. One year our younger daughter took a big boxful home and put together four neatly organized albums for her dad's birthday, but that was the last attempt at order. Let's just say that I was never attracted to this scrap-booking craze that has sparked the creativity of a lot of women.

I know from past experience that there's a drawback to this project. I'll sort through all those memories of the happy, busy years and wallow in depression. I hung up on my mother one hectic, stressful day when I called looking for sympathy and she told me that someday I'd look back and realize these were the best years of my life. But she was right.

So I'll set aside a few pictures that'll bring me back to reality. Like those snapshots of a carefree beach vacation. I'll remind myself that the kids weren't speaking to me all the way home because I'd insisted that on the last day they take their beach pails down the lane and pick wild blackberries to take home for jelly. And that when we got home I had to wipe sand out of the bottom of the washer for three days.

There's Luanne in her tutu and slippers, scowling dreadfully because she'd wanted to quit ballet for months. That was her last recital, incidentally.

There's three-year-old Matt and his cousin on a camping trip, tennis shoes shining wetly because we'd just fished the two kids out of the creek. They only wanted to see if the watermelon we'd placed there was cold yet, they explained.

There's little Katy, arms raised and face contorted in what I thought were giggles, until her now-grown siblings reminded me it was a prize-winning tantrum.

There's toddler Shawn, knee up on the table as he admires his candy-loaded choo-choo train birthday cake. The next shot would have shown his face in the caboose.

I'll fill disks for all the kids. Maybe they'll be drawn into all those childhood memories and it'll make up for the fact that they're not left with much else.

August, 2010

CAN A FUNERAL BE HUMOROUS?

When we had our wills made recently, it brought to mind another depressing subject: funerals. But I must have been in a perverse mood that day, because pretty soon I was thinking about humorous ones. Yes, there can be such a thing as a funny, if slightly warped, funeral.

We've probably all been to one where the presiding clergy not only mispronounces the deceased's name, but describes a person nothing like the one we knew. My Uncle Ted's eulogy was so different from the lifelong hot-tempered, cranky man I remembered that it seemed he should have been swept up to heaven before he even died, like the perfect Enoch in the Old Testament. It gave me a little hope that maybe the same thing will happen at my funeral, and family members will forget that the grandkids learned their first bad words from Grandma. Nobody will remember that I could carry a grudge forever, and have hissy-fits when things didn't go my way.

But it's the funeral with a mispronounced name that worries me. It makes me think I should abandon my religion, "Reading the Sunday Paper over a Leisurely Breakfast," and start going to church before I get any older, so some stranger doesn't call me "Shofeld" in my final rites.

Then there was the funeral of a young man who'd been estranged from his family for years. His sister said his favorite song was "Stairway to Heaven," and they must have thought the title had a spiritual ring to it, so they found a CD to play at the funeral. Unfortunately, the song is done by Led Zeppelin, ends in a high-tempo hard-rock section, and the shortest version is eight minutes long. Everybody sat peeking at each other out of the corner of their eyes while it went on and on, and the funeral director cast uneasy glances around, obviously trying to decide if he should pull the plug.

My mother's memorial service had a bright spot…bright to the point of garishness. It was scheduled for mid-afternoon in Vancouver, and our younger daughter decided she had time that morning to get the usual rinse to bring out coppery highlights in her hair. Something went terribly wrong in that stylist's chair. Her hair was so Little Orphan Annie orange it could stop traffic. She got lots of curious stares in the first part of her drive, so she whipped into The Dalles and threw herself on the mercy of a walk-in beauty salon. It helped, but not enough. She arrived just in time for the service, with hair still bright enough to light up the chapel.

Dad passed away before Mom, and his funeral had even more mishaps.

It began when I insisted that the prelude be not religious music, but the old songs Dad loved. Since my rebel cousin Hazel was the church organist, she agreed. Instead of the familiar hymns, we heard songs I remembered him singing in my childhood like "Love's Old Sweet Song," "Down in the Valley," "Home Sweet Home" and "Beautiful Dreamer." Other people might not have approved, but I know Dad did. I felt his nearness in those songs, so maybe that wasn't a mishap. But it got worse.

When I received the call about Dad, I took off right away to be with Mom, and Russ followed later with the proper clothing for both of us. The day of the funeral was hectic, and when I slipped on my shoes at the last minute, I realized that although they were both black, one was shiny patent leather and the other wasn't. And one had a higher heel than the other. Mom's shoes were so bunion-stretched that they'd have fallen off, so I just had to walk carefully, hoping the relatives I hadn't seen for ages wouldn't think I'd developed a gimp over the years…and REALLY hoping they didn't look at my feet.

The reason it had been so hectic at home was that Russ didn't have the pants to go with his suit coat. At arrival he had hung the two items, on separate hangers, on the hallway rod. Mom hung Dad's clothes on the same rod. When the undertaker called for the clothing, she grabbed the right jacket and the wrong pants. Poor Russ made a frantic pre-funeral run to the closest mall to find a pair of slacks that hopefully matched his suit coat. They didn't. With his mismatched suit and my mismatched shoes, we made a lovely pair.

The undertaker was a family friend, and he later commented, "Well, we had to cut the pants open all the way down the rear and the back of the legs to make them fit, but I knew the family was stressed and didn't want to bother you."

With his wry sense of humor, Dad must have loved getting the last laugh. I'll bet he chuckled all the way up that "Stairway to Heaven." And he probably reached his destination humming "Love's Old Sweet Song" in his beautiful tenor.

September, 2010

THERE'S NO SUCH THING AS TOO MANY TOYS!

I seem to have a hard time knowing when enough is enough. Putting it as kindly as possible, I just don't know when to quit.

After our son and daughter-in-law moved from Berkeley to Seattle, where we'll be able to see our two-year-old grandson often, I got carried away. I finessed my eBay bidding, sitting at the computer with my fingers poised on the keys so I could swoop in when there was less than a minute left on the auction, and wouldn't be out-bid. What I couldn't find on eBay, Craigslist, or yard sales was readily available at Toys R Us or my favorite website, Fisher-Price for Grandmas. The backyard looks like an upscale daycare center, and they haven't even made their first visit to Yakima yet.

It's really not my fault, it's the vendors'. They shouldn't put such good prices on such cute stuff. Who could resist the child-size Cherry Blossom Market, with its grocery cart, cash register and all that pretend food?

When you can get a toddler's first ride-on, battery-operated police car with siren and flashing lights for $35.00 and free shipping, wouldn't it be just plain silly not to buy it?

And that yard sale little table and chairs set that just needed a simple refinishing job…don't tell me I'm the only grandma who would throw her body across the table and grab both chairs in a death grip to make sure somebody else didn't get it.

My personality is just as flawed in the sewing room. I was going to sew Jasper a couple of pairs of cotton shorts for summer play…just a couple. But when I saw how little fabric a pair of size two shorts requires, and what colorful remnants I had stashed away, well, darn it! I ended up with 11 pairs. I soothe my conscience by telling myself that since they're potty-training Jasper, he'll probably go though three or four pairs a day, easy.

I finally got the quiet activity book done. Unfortunately, I kept thinking of things to add to the basic pattern. When we play with his

Happy Sounds House, Jasper's favorite thing is taking pretend clothes out of the dryer and folding them. So I made a page that has a laundry basket for clothes, and a dryer with a door that opens so he can put the clothes in it. Then, of course, there had to be clothes. So I ironed on Pellon to make the fabric stiff enough to last awhile, and made jeans, shorts, shirts and pajamas in miniature Daddy, Mommy and Jasper sizes. He'll love it.

However, when I got to the last stage of the project - sewing all the pages and the cover together down the middle seam - I made a shocking discovery…too many pages. It was too thick for my sewing machine. It was also too thick for a shoe repairman's machine. When I carried it into the saddle and tack repair shop, I got some funny looks, but his machine did the trick. That book is bound to stay bound!

I learned that I also bite off more than Grandpa and I can chew when I plan activities. We took Jasper to the zoo in Seattle while his parents unpacked, and both of us ended the day so exhausted we barely made it to the comfort of the car in the parking lot. We should have spread it over several days. They don't make zoos like they used to, with cruel cages clustered together. The animals, of course, are much happier to have an African Savannah, an Asian Tropical Forest, a North American Woodland. But there was so much walking that by the end of the day I was envying people trapped in wheelchairs. And it wasn't just walking, it was running. At the first hint of a coming attraction, Jasper bailed out of his stroller with no warning and took off at warp speed, with us following. He never ran out of energy.

It was the same at the Seattle Children's Museum. Jasper hit the ground running and never slowed down. There were enough attractions to keep him on the go for three hours, and once again we barely made it to the car afterward.

So I'm going to change my ways. Less is more. A kid enjoys playing in the empty box as much as the toy that came in it. Rome wasn't built in a day. Surely a tech can figure out a way to lock me out of eBay. Six double pages is definitely enough for a quiet book, and it doesn't require binding at a saddle and tack shop. Slow and easy wins the day.

Okay, so I made up most of those adages. Adages are wisdom, and you can't overdo on wisdom!

September, 2010

SEVENTY'S THE NEW FORTY…NOT!

Recently, I was asked to speak at an informal coffee-klatsch type meeting of senior citizens at a church, and decided to talk about the joys of growing older. Then I thought…wait a minute, that'd only take about three minutes. I don't want to put on a girdle and earrings for a three-minute talk. So I decided to also cover the un-joys of growing older.

I never planned to get old, but oh, well…Like I swore I'd never do, I'll hold onto Russ's arm when the driveway is icy, and probably pull him down with me so we have his-and-her matching broken hips. I'll pick up my magnifying glass when I'm reading the small print in the yard sale ads. We'll both smile and nod and pretend we heard what the other one was saying, even if it sometimes earns a disbelieving stare when he says something like, "Have you read the obituary page yet? John Harris died." And I nod, smile and say, "Isn't that nice?"

Getting old follows a gradual downhill path. When our children are babies, just the sight of mommy or daddy's face brings big, drooly smiles. When they're toddlers, we can do anything. We can kiss an owie and make it better. After a scary dream, we can lift the bedspread, look under the bed and say firmly, "Go away, monster!" and it goes.

When they start school, their teacher pushes us off the pedestal. She is now the fountain of knowledge.

Then they reach the teen years, and Mom and Dad are both dumb as rocks. Our music makes them gag. They pretend they don't know us if they're with their friends and run into us at the mall.

They become adults, and we enter the years when you bite your lip and chew the inside of your cheek to keep your mouth shut. When they bring home a fellow who has "deadbeat loser" written all over him, or a girl that you instinctively know would provide you with grandbabies who always smell like throw-up and have a pacifier tied around their neck until kindergarten, you just smile blandly and say "How nice to meet you." Because there's a good chance they'll be in family pictures from now on, although sometimes you go through the photo albums years later with the scissors and leave a little hole where their face was. (I'm grateful our son married late. He waited for just the right woman...no sour grandbabies and dangling pacifiers in this family!)

After a few years, you regain a little stature in your kids' eyes, when their kids start putting them through the paces. But you never, ever, say "I told you so."

There are some sad inconsistencies about growing old.

1. Women find they don't have to shave their legs as often. But that isn't a blessing, because your body uses that hair-making process to transfer the hairs to your chin, at the time when your eyesight makes them harder to find with the tweezers.
2. Men lose that nice firm little rear-end that looked so good when they were young. It just sort of fades away, and they have to cinch their belt up to avoid the droopy-drawers look of gang-bangers. Unfortunately, sometimes that rear plumpness stays in the family. It transfers to the wife, where it's not nearly as cute.
3. While your bones get so fragile that you're afraid to walk on ice, your toenails gain the texture of moose antlers, and you need a hatchet and chainsaw for your pedicure.
4. You finally have time to read all you want, and you learn that many of the modern best-sellers are not your cup of tea. You have to choose carefully. And quite often you'll get to chapter three before you realize why you checked out this book. It looked good to you on the library shelf just like it did the first time you saw it. And it took you three chapters to realize the plot is awfully familiar. But that's okay. You've pretty much forgotten what you read the first time, so you can enjoy it again.

There are a few good things about growing old:

1. You can take a nap in the daytime without feeling guilty.
2. When you look back on the good old days, nostalgia has painted everything golden.
3. You can accept life's little disappointments when they inevitably come along, because you see the bigger picture. You've dealt with harder things, and learned the bitter lessons they bring.

4. You can be thankful for the quiet joys: sharing life with someone you've been with so long that they feel like part of you, knowing you'll take care of him as he will take care of you.
5. Last, and most important: Growing old beats the alternative, hands down!

October, 2010

GOING SISSY-CAMPING IN AN RV

We thought we might be in time to get a few huckleberries, so we went camping with the two grandkids, two daughters, and our older daughter's friend Lavonne, at Peterson's Prairie, in the Trout Lake/Mt. Adams area. It's the site of many happy trips of the past. By this I mean happy for the rest of the family.

I'm not the outdoor type. I slogged along on camping trips for many years because it was a mother's duty to provide enjoyment for her children.

So why did I try camping again? I wish I could say that it was because I stopped being a sissy, but that would be lying. This trip was in our older daughter and her friend's RV...camping FOR sissies.

We started off well, planning to leave between four and four-thirty p.m., and actually leaving at four-fifteen. That in itself was historic. We laughed and talked all the way to the crucial signpost pointing the way to Peterson's Prairie.

"Fourteen miles!" my husband exclaimed. "That can't be right!" But signs don't lie.

Soon the road got rougher, with Russ periodically shaking his head and muttering comments about how nothing looked familiar. Darkness began to fall. He directed the driver, our daughter's friend Lavonne, to turn off on a road that at least angled in the right direction. When the road became a narrow graveled washboard, she said, "This can't be the way to an established park!" There was no place to turn around so someone got out with a flashlight to guide her as she backed the RV down the way we had come.

"Look, a campfire!" someone shouted. We edged across a little bridge, dodged ruts in a forest path, and pulled up in front of the campsite. Russ got out to ask directions.

"They must plan to camp a long time," granddaughter Caity said. "They've got a living room couch by the fire."

A moment of reflective silence, and then our daughter Luanne spoke up. "If a person wanted to cook meth, this would be the perfect place."

Eventually Russ returned, with news that the men were from California and didn't know the area. Lavonne capably got us turned around, a feat somewhat like fitting a semi into a motorcycle parking space in the dark, if the space is surrounded by big trees and full of holes and stumps. We waited until we were out of gunshot range before stopping so Russ and Lavonne could study the map the campers had given him. It was either out of date or possibly from another state.

The odometer showed we'd traveled more than 14 miles, so we headed back to the store we'd passed just before that fateful road sign, for directions.

The road sign said 1/4 mile, not 14. Sure enough, 1/4 mile past the sign was a road branching off with an arrow marked "Peterson's Prairie," hidden by drooping fir branches.

We found our site, turned on the generator, and heated up supper in the microwave. Then the generator was turned off, since the battery would provide light enough to get to bed. We'd eaten a few bites when the lights went out. Luanne clicked the generator switch, with no results. Finally Russ suggested that if the battery was dead, maybe the RV motor had to be turned on to start the generator. That worked. New rule: don't use the microwave when you're not hooked up. It's a power hog.

Our daughter Katy arrived from Portland. She'd left home about the time we were wandering down gravel roads, and found us with no problem. Said she'd just Googled Washington Parks and got directions. With a dark look at Russ, Lavonne said, "We had Google Grandpa."

While breakfast dishes were being washed next morning, Katy remarked that water was standing in the shower and starting to run down the hall.

Lavonne and Luanne opened drain valves, with no result, so they drove to Trout Lake and bought a plunger, plumber's snake and drain cleaner. Still plugged. Then they noticed a valve on the kitchen side of the RV, opposite from the others. When that valve was opened, gray water gushed out. They turned it off and drove to the closest RV dump station, where the kitchen water of four previous trips poured out. All those trips had been to parks with RV hookups, and when hoses were hooked up and they heard water gurgling out, they'd thought the job was done. Yes, it had emptied the shower and toilet water, but not kitchen.

The rest of the time was fairly uneventful, if you overlook four or five different types of snores echoing in a small space. There was a little flurry of alarm that night when somebody smelled gas. After all the burners were checked, the owners of the RV finally told their guests to open the windows, shut up and go to sleep.

We were grateful to wake up next morning. Near death made the huckleberry pancakes taste even better. Four of the group had spent an hour and a half in the fields and brought back a pint of huckleberries.

The trip wasn't in vain. We got a few huckleberries!

October, 2010

IT'S GOT TO BE ME, OR HARRY & DAVID

You'd think a marriage of 50-plus years would last forever. We've done so much adjusting that we're nothing like the people we were all those years ago when we got married. We wouldn't recognize those 18 and 20 year-olds if we met them on the street.

I've learned to ask an occasional stupid question when he's watching baseball, basketball or football, so he'll think I'm at least aware, if not interested. He's learned to chuckle, or at least smile once in a while when I'm watching British comedies, so I'll think he's enjoying the program.

We've adjusted to each other's relatives, even learned to love some of them.

We've gone through the skimping and sacrificing part of marriage…the search for coins under the sofa cushions for a gallon of milk at the end of the month; endless camping trips because that was all we could afford for a vacation; moonlighting or part-time work in addition to regular jobs to bring in extra money.

I've seen him through serious illnesses and surgeries. He's seen me through PMS, cranky pregnancies and menopause.

Even the stress of raising four kids couldn't break us up. Oh, who am I kidding? The four kids probably strengthened the union. We'd have been afraid of getting sole custody. Without a partner, how can you trick the kids with the bad cop, good cop routine? You'd have to be bad cop all the time. Who could take turns missing work when a child is sick? And what about that "Go ask your mother" and "You'll have to talk to your dad about that" bit. You'd have to make all the decisions all the time. Worst of all, who'd be there to say, "Don't talk nonsense. Of course you're a good mother (or father, as the case may be). It's not our fault." No, I definitely can't blame it on the four children.

Things went well right up to the introduction of Harry and David. No, they don't run a "gentlemen's club" or a porn web site. They're the company in southern Oregon that features a fruit-of-the-month club, and tasty condiments like Harry and David's Pepper and Onion Relish. We buy it by the case. When we're getting ready to go to Portland, we have to check the pantry to see how many jars are left, so we can stop at their shop in the Troutdale outlet mall. Russ's love affair with the stuff is threatening me in my personal comfort zone.

Oh, piffle, you might be thinking. What a minor problem. Ranks right up there with the husband always putting the toilet paper roll on backward. But this is important.

I'm a good cook. That's not bragging, that's just stating fact. Even the most mediocre of us has one good trait, and that's mine. It's not the strong point I would have chosen. I'd have preferred a scientific mind that would discover the cure for cancer, or a metabolism that turns calories into energy and skips right over that storing fat for future needs thing, but I wasn't given a choice. Being a good cook is the strong point I was stuck with, and I just have to make the best of it.

I once came home with a blue ribbon from the Central Washington Fair, and I've been a winner in some magazine recipe contests. But the recipe Russ admires is the sandwich wrap I made up, consisting of sliced turkey, melted Pepperjack cheese, and liberal smears of Harry and David's Pepper and Onion Relish.

At first I could ignore his obsession. Sure, scrambled eggs could be spiced with Harry and David as well as by Heinz Catsup. If a layer of Harry and David made a bland casserole more appealing to him, fine. Go for it. Then he began to step over the line.

When, after several tries, I've finally re-created the salmon with cranberry hazelnut glaze that we loved at a Canadian restaurant, and he plops a glob of Harry and David on his serving, he has veered off into dangerous territory. When he dribbles Harry and David over my pineapple glazed ham with citrus chutney, I look across the table and realize I'm seeing a stranger. But the straw that broke the camel's back was when he garnished my long-time family favorite chicken tortilla casserole with Harry and David instead of homemade fresh salsa.

In a last-ditch attempt to save our marriage (and because we're too cheap for couples counseling), I'm trying one last desperate measure. I'm not cooking all next week. Instead I'll set his place at the table with a bowl, spoon, and jar of Harry and David's Pepper and Onion Relish. I hope that by next Sunday he'll have eaten his fill of it.

If not, it's time for the big guns. I'll e-mail Dr. Phil. After all, you can't toss 55 years into the dumpster.

December, 2010

MUSIC BRINGS IT BACK

Thanks to the internet, I finally found a song for which I've spent years searching. I paid the ninety-nine cents to record it from a web site featuring the singing of two young sisters, and added it to my all-time favorite Christmas mixed CD.

It's "Winds through the Olive Trees." The girls have sweet, childish voices, sounding ten or eleven years old. That's as it should be. I first heard it many years ago, sung at a school Christmas program by kids about that age.

My husband began teaching elementary school back in those golden years when schools had Christmas programs, not winter festivals. Often they staged a nativity scene, and if the religious music bothered a few folks, they were kind enough to let their neighbors enjoy it.

For years, the school Christmas program marked the season for our family as much as the homemade Advent calendar and felt stockings I sewed.

That very first elementary school program was an important event for us. I dressed two-year-old Luanne in her little red jumper and ruffled tights, and donned the red velvet maternity top my sister-in-law passed on to me when she gave birth a few weeks earlier. Luanne received lots of chucking-under-the-chin and "Oh, what a darling little girl!" gushing. It was hard to pretend modesty. After all, she WAS a darling little girl!

The 6th grade narrator must have had some theatrical blood in his veins. He did the job right. When he got to an important part of the narration, his "Mary was GR-E-A-T with child" made it hard to stay straight-faced. There was a lot of strangled coughing to cover the laughter, because he sounded just like the new Tony the Tiger cereal commercials that appeared on everyone's fishbowl-shaped TV screen. The lady behind us patted my shoulder, acknowledging my own greatness with child. Our son Matthew was born a month later.

Those programs stopped for us when Russ moved from elementary school to junior high. We didn't miss them, though, because we had our own kids' Christmas events to attend through the years. When our youngest son, Shawn, told us it was silly to come because he wasn't really singing, just moving his lips, it didn't stop us. It was tradition.

We went on to high school choir performances, and even to a college Christmas program when our younger daughter, Katy, was in the choir at Linfield College. We went without concerts for a few years, and then the grandkids were in school and we started the tradition all over again.

But the event that sticks in my memory is the one in our family room out at the farm. Matt, ten and Katy, four, had been working on some hush-hush project for days when Matt told us we were invited to a special Christmas program they'd prepared. I'm sorry to say that, even busier than usual, I put them off for a while.

I knew something was up when they asked if they could use some red and green construction paper and Elmer's glue. And where could they find the silver stars left over from my ill-fated attempt at a chore list? They needed them.

At dinnertime Russ and I were presented with a combination invitation/program agenda. I still have it in a scrapbook along with a Polaroid picture of the event, which took place the next evening. You can't ignore a written invitation.

They'd water-colored an impressive backdrop from the roll of newsprint I kept for boring rainy-day projects, which explained the stains on the card table where the color seeped through.

Matt improvised a Santa costume of red sweatshirt, cotton beard, stocking cap, and a gunnysack full of wadded-up newspapers, with a few brightly-wrapped empty gift boxes on top.

Katy wore her Sunday best. She sang a couple of carols, including "Winds Through the Olive Trees," which she'd heard me sing over the years. The best features of the song are that it's simple to remember, and it's pitched low enough that you don't have to be an opera diva to sing it.

Matt did a hand-puppet show and played the piano. One song was "There is a Tavern in the Town," which he'd learned to play by ear after hearing my dad sing it. Following the title on the program was written, "It's not a Christmas song, but Christmas is a little bit of everything."

They gave Shawn a brief walk-on part; he was too young to rely on for a speaking role. He was the little boy who listened when Santa read "The Night Before Christmas." Luanne, our oldest child, had hostess duty. She served the cookies I'd been instructed to bake, and poured the red Kool-Aid.

Now when I hear "Winds through the Olive Trees," I remember that first Christmas program in the crowded Roosevelt School gym. And better still, I remember sitting in the old farmhouse family room while Matt and Katy proudly presented their Christmas spectacular.

I think I'll dig out that Polaroid picture before I play the song again.

December, 2010

DECORATING'S FUN…UNDECORATING ISN'T

Ah…(imagine a mournful sigh)…it's almost time to take the Christmas decorations down. We usually do the job on New Year's Day, with Russ working really fast on TV commercials and much slower the rest of the time. He multi-tasks by watching the football game at the same time. I multi-task by giving many sad sighs while I work, and making trips to the kitchen to stir the Hoppin' John. It's a traditional southern meal for New Year's Day. The black-eyed peas and ham dish is supposed to bring good luck throughout the year. Russ spices his up with Harry & David's Pepper Onion Relish, of course, but I take mine straight.

I always hate to let go of Christmas. One year after we started using an artificial tree, I decided Christmas wasn't over until I SAID it was over. The tree stayed up, and I watched Christmas videos until mid-January. The videotaped versions of the original Grinch and Rudolph TV specials are a little more golden each time I play them, because I remember Russ and I watching them on TV with the kids when they were small. It was a holiday tradition we reluctantly dropped only when they became too grown-up to humor us any longer. (Well, maybe I was the only reluctant one.) I probably would have hung onto Christmas until Valentine's Day, had our grown kids not started giving me uneasy looks when they caught me watching "The Muppet's Christmas Carol" or "Emmett Otter's Jug-Band Christmas.

So we'll undecorate at a sensible time this year. The job would be a lot easier if I could force myself to adopt a "less is more" lifestyle. Once in awhile I purge the holiday closet, usually regretting it afterward. If I ever write my autobiography, the title will be *If it's Missing, I Sold it at a Yard Sale.*

I searched in vain for the patchwork wreaths I made years ago, before remembering that last year I decided the front of the house had gone from gaily decorated to tacky. I aimed for modern elegance, and sold all my homemade efforts at our yard sale. Unfortunately, patchwork wreaths went perfectly with the plywood polar bears and penguins Russ made so long ago, and there's no way those animals weren't going to grace the front yard!

This was the first year two-year-old grandson Jasper was at our house for Christmas, so we pulled out all the stops. Those lovable critters had to be the first thing Jasper saw after his eyesight adjusted to the glare of the outdoor lights. Since electricity rates skyrocketed, we had older grandson Steve wait until shortly before Christmas to string them on every surface that had a hook. Russ and I winced every time we switched them on at twilight and saw the indoor lights dim momentarily.

I kicked myself for selling those patchwork wreaths. Their bright color would have pleased Jasper much more than elegant evergreens. And who am I kidding? If I haven't achieved elegance by the time I'm this old, it's never going to happen.

So I went to the opposite of elegance…back to the Old-Fashioned Grandma Décor look. I plastered bright Santa clings to the windows, and hauled out the little wooden sleds and their teddy bear riders to go on the shelves within Jasper's reach. On a low table I arranged the ethnic nativity scene the daughters got me a couple of years ago at a Fair Trade bazaar. The chubby felt figures are stuffed with cotton, and I figured if it was tough enough for those kids in Kyrgyzstan, it should survive a two-year-old. I didn't bother making snow-covered mountains out of cans covered with fluffy cotton, or nestling the yurt/manger in a snowy hillside, as I usually do. I knew they wouldn't survive Hurricane Jasper. The village houses went up on the mantel, where Jasper could admire them only in the arms of a patient parent, grandparent or auntie, of which he has plenty.

I shouldn't be so reluctant to let Christmas go this time. This year I stuck to my resolve to not be sewing or wrapping gifts until dawn of Christmas morning, so I had more time to enjoy the inelegant, homemade ambience. The women of the family took over the cooking, although they did allow me to make a couple of new recipes I'd been wanting to try. Handing over the alpha female role is a little sad, but I don't want to be like Queen Elizabeth and hang onto the job until the heir to the throne is too old to remember which part of England he's prince of.

So I enjoyed Christmas, but it's time to bring the house back to normal. One relic is going to remain, though. It's the tiny handprint on the glass sliding door that separates the sewing room from the rest of the house. Jasper knows that's where the toys are kept. He left his mark.

Going back to Old-Fashioned Grandma Décor must have been successful. I learned later that as they pulled out of the driveway, Jasper said wistfully, "I miss their house."

I guess that'll hold me until next Christmas.

February, 2011

EVERY KID NEEDS A BOOK LIGHT

I recently learned that for a two-and-a-half year old, a $9.99 book-light outscores a truckload of Christmas toys. Santa could have saved a ton of money!

We just spent a weekend in Seattle. It'd been almost a whole month since we last saw grandson Jasper, and I still hadn't made it through withdrawal, so we braved Snoqualmie Pass.

We usually take a toy, but this time we didn't. I mean, how can any new toy make an impression after Christmas? Besides, I was curious to see if he greeted us with as much joy when we were empty-handed.

We learned a lot during the weekend, and so did Jasper.

Seattle Children's Museum is old hat now, so we wanted to take him to the one in Bellevue. We buckled him into his safety seat and decided to take the route Russ was familiar with, rather than the shorter one our son Shawn described, that had a lot of new directions. It took us an hour to get through the University District to I-5. While sitting bumper to bumper, Russ said mournfully, "B-A-A-D choice."

Jasper's in that stage of wanting to know what everything means. "What's bad choice?" he asked. I explained it was when you decided to do the wrong thing.

"What Grandpa DO?" he asked, gazing at him with interest, probably seeing a time-out or a stern scolding in the offing.

"He chose the wrong route," I replied. That, of course, required the definition of route. Also I-5 and rush hour traffic. The drive was a learning experience for all three of us.

Next day, after a prior warning, Jasper's dad told him that if he threw a toy in the house one more time, it would be taken away from him. In response, he clobbered the Fisher-Price race track with it, and it was confiscated. Over his sobs I said, "Boy, did you ever make a B-A-A-D choice!" He chuckled through his tears, then moved on.

But back to the book light. As soon as we returned from the Bellevue museum, Jasper hurried into the bedroom where we'd put our luggage, probably looking for a Macy's shopping bag, which is what his toys usually arrive in.

"What's this?" he called excitedly, and emerged holding my reading-in-bed book-light. I explained, then hung it around his neck and clicked the two lights on.

He wore it for the rest of the visit. Periodically I'd hear a small voice calling from his darkened room, "Grandma, it's time to read books in the dark!" That night I removed it after he fell asleep, so I could read in bed.

It wasn't just for reading in the dark, though. He's heavily into pretending, where he makes up the scenario and assigns your role. When we played library, the book light became the scanner that he carefully passed over the bar-codes on the books, after scanning my library card. (Which had been a wallet calendar in its previous existence.) It was the projector when we played movie theatre, while he shook dice in a Tupperware container for the popcorn machine. We made shadow puppets. It was the spotlight when he identified the planets decorating his bedroom wall. It was the scanner when his toy kitchen turned into a grocery store. He shone it under the couch and used his toy broom to round up missing Fisher-Price Little People.

The weekend reminded me that kids can find fun in the simplest things, and imagination beats Toys R Us, hands down.

I remembered tea parties with my dolls and my Grandma Hubbard, using pieces of broken crockery for dishes and a Mason jar for a teapot. Grandma provided the butter and sugar sandwiches, cut into dainty quarters for the event.

I remembered the dollhouses Mom and I made when I was little. They were small cardboard boxes, with furniture, décor and family members cut from the Sears catalog and attached to the walls. Lots of flour and water paste went into that project.

I remembered my kids going through old magazines, cutting out items that illustrated each letter of the alphabet and pasting them into a cheap dime-store scrapbook. We'd progressed to Elmer's Glue by then.

I remembered the refrigerator box that became a ship and a house. Stood on end, it was a rocket ship. Battered and sagging, its final role was a department store elevator.

Of course, we all remember riding on a train that was a row of kitchen chairs, and tents and forts made of blankets draped between chairs.

Shawn, Becky and Jasper will be over for a visit in a couple of weeks. I think I'll have ready a collection of empty boxes, old magazines, blunt kiddy scissors and Elmer's Washable School Glue.

Oh, almost forgot the most important item. I'll buy him a book light of his own to take home. He'll dream up all kinds of new uses for it, with his dad and mom playing supporting roles!

March 2010

FLUFFING PILLOWS AND READING STORIES

Oh, what fun! I've got a sick kid home to take care of, after all these years.

No, I'm not a sadist. I don't enjoy seeing people suffer. There's just something in me that enjoys serving ice water with a bent straw, fluffing pillows, and digging out the most appealing books and magazines for a sick kid.

Never mind that this sick kid is old enough that if I told her age she'd probably whap me upside the head when she's back on her feet. And she's not sick, just recuperating from a little operation that was supposed to be a walk in the park, same-day-surgery on her hand that turned out to be more like a stroll through a minefield than a walk in the park. Instead of childhood's countless games of Old Maid (with the sufferer winning, of course), the challenge is figuring out how to suspend her arm from the bed's headboard. And instead of requesting the red Kool-Aid or ginger ale that went with those long ago sicknesses, she'd be asking for something stronger if she wasn't on pain medication.

Still, it brings back memories of menthol-scented vaporizers and vile berry-flavored antibiotics, of green Jello and chicken-noodle soup (unfortunately made by Campbell instead of me). It brings back Viewmaster slides projected on the bedroom wall, stories read aloud, and the recovery that allowed graduation from the bed to the living room couch, where the patient watched TV from a sea of pillows.

With four kids, when a virus or even the common cold came to our house, it settled in for a long stay (the virus, not the kids…well, them too, I guess). Back then there were no immunizations for some of the childhood diseases, like chicken pox. When that first pimply-looking thing appeared, you knew you were in it for the long haul. One spring my sister-in-law said she'd spent the entire time between Christmas and Easter playing board games with poxy kids, dining for lunch on the broth left from their chicken-noodle soup and the crusts from their peanut butter and jelly sandwiches.

Our two older children and two younger ones were separated by enough years that often we had the déjà vu experience of going through the same illnesses twice, years apart. I'd have to remind myself that these two preferred grape popsicles and Dr. Pepper, not the cherry popsicles and ginger ale the older two asked for when they were sick.

Sometimes, though, they'd all be sick at the same time, which meant changing many sheets and pajamas in the middle of the night, and playing Musical Beds to provide changes of scenery. When they got to the couch and pillows stage, it meant deciding which two got opposite ends of the couch, who got the recliner, and who got a cozy pillow-nest on the floor. Also, whose turn it was to choose the TV program.

It also meant keeping track of which kid wanted to turn her face to the wall and not be disturbed, and which one requested that grandma's little hand-bell be put on the night-stand, so he wouldn't have to strain his voice for service. The cheery "ding" of that little bell turned out to be every bit as annoying when rung by a young hand as when grandma clanged it during her recuperation at our house.

The daughter sleeping now with her arm hanging from the headboard never demanded a lot of TLC. Even years ago, when her little Volkswagen challenged a logging truck on black ice and she fractured several vertebrae, she wasn't demanding. We played a lot of Scrabble during her hospitalization and by then, I didn't have to let her win…we were a fair match. Wrapping her cast in Saran for a quick shower was a challenge. Even more of a challenge was figuring out how to shampoo her waist-length hair. Her wedding was six months in the future, and she wanted to keep her long hair until then. We finally managed by having her climb up on the kitchen counter and stretch out with her legs resting on the stove-top and her head over the sink, but supported by a tall can of V-8 juice. It wasn't pretty, and it wasn't approved by the American Medical Association, but it worked.

So here I am, remembering old times. I never played Betsy McCall paper dolls on the bedspread with this daughter, like I did with the younger one. She never whined, "I'm bored! What shall I do?" like her two-years-younger brother. As soon as she started to feel better, she just wanted to be up and at it. She's the one who went back to school the day she broke the thermometer testing the temperature of the inside of a freshly-baked chocolate chip cookie. I figured if she was ready for scientific experiments, she was ready for school.

But she did enjoy being read to. I think I'll dig out those *Little House* books by Laura Ingalls Wilder. Maybe she'll let me read to her when she wakes up.

May 2011

THE FAMILY ROCKING CHAIR, PART TWO

A baby from the next generation is being rocked in the old family rocking chair: our great-grandson, Roman Nathaniel Pietsch.

It was the first piece of furniture we bought. Our older daughter was an infant when we prowled the second-hand stores down by the harbor in Bellingham, and squeezed two dollars from the grocery budget to buy it. Russ and I could sit on the sway-backed couch that came with our furnished apartment near the college. It had springs that could cause a serious stab wound in the rear unless you positioned the "Souvenir of Vancouver, B.C." pillow just right before you sat down. That took care of the problem. But a baby needed to be rocked.

I don't know how many generations had already known the soothing effects of the chair when we bought it, but it served all four of our kids, then our older daughter's two. Most recently it rocked Jasper, our two-and-a-half-year-old grandson. Jasper's mommy and daddy hauled it over from Seattle when our oldest grandchild, Caity, and her husband Trevor announced that they were expecting. Now Roman Nathaniel Pietsch gets rocked in the family chair.

It's hard to believe that Caity, the granddaughter who brought me so much joy as a baby, can have one of her own. Our daughter, Caity's mom, can't possibly be aware of the years of happiness little Roman brings with him. When I hold this tiny, soft, peacefully-sleeping bundle, I can't even picture him getting into the mischief he'll find in a couple of years, like his cousin Jasper does. But that's part of the enjoyment, seeing intelligence form and personality grow, even when that personality includes the occasional tantrum and rock-hard determination…balanced by the delight in his voice when he says, "Hi, Grandma!" and runs to hug me around the knees.

When I remember the fun I had (and still have) with grandchildren, I remind myself that it's our older daughter's turn now. She's the grandma, and I'm a grandma-once-removed. There's a herd of grandmas, honorary grandmas, and great-grandmas, so poor

Roman might have a problem keeping them all straight. I hope the others of my generation haven't already called dibs on the title, "Gee-Gee" (for great-grandma). If they have, maybe we'll just have to be Gee-Gee D, Gee-Gee L and Gee-Gee M. We'll have to excuse Roman if he decides any kindly-looking woman over the age of 50 (some WAY over) is to be treated like a grandma.

But back to the chair. We just spent the weekend with grandson Jasper, former occupant of the family chair. We took along a sturdy child's rocker I'd found on the Internet. He loved it.

When we visit we get the master bedroom, and Becky and Shawn sleep in their son's room. Becky said she woke early next morning to soft noise. Jasper was rocking in his new chair, murmuring quietly to himself (or maybe an imaginary friend). She couldn't get all the words, but she did hear "Grandma and Grandpa" a couple of times.

When we first presented the chair to him, Jasper rocked in it for a minute, then lit up with an expression illustrated in the comic strips by a light bulb over the character's head. "Hey," he exclaimed, "my mommy's got a chair that rocks like this!" He hopped off and went searching for the chair that he hadn't missed for almost a year. We explained that baby Roman's mommy was using it now.

He didn't protest, but I'm kind of worried. During the visit it was time to return his all-time favorite book to the library. The tale of Foo Frog and Su-Lin Salamander has kept him enthralled for many weeks, and he didn't want to give it up. "Just let me take it to the library and talk to the lady," his mommy said. "I think she'll let me renew it one more time." Explaining the term "renewing" didn't solve the problem. Neither did our offer to go to Barnes and Noble and buy another copy. A trip there revealed that they didn't have the book, so the fate of Foo Frog and Su-Lin Salamander was dropped. The library trip was postponed, but Jasper carried the book around all afternoon, and when he rocked in his little chair, he sat on the book, evidently not trusting any of us. As soon as we got home, I ordered a copy from Amazon to be sent directly to him. His parents reported that the highlight of Jasper's day came when he saw his name being written in black ink inside the book that was his forever.

The reason I'm a little worried is that Shawn, Becky and Jasper haven't been over to see the new baby yet. I'm wondering if Jasper will search for the family rocker and try to haul it out of their house on his little two-and-a-half-year-old back, wailing piteously, "No, don't take it away! I NEED it!" like he did with the library book. Could be a bit awkward.

May, 2011

HOME EC FOR THE DOMESTICALLY CHALLENGED

The class has a fancier name now, but back when I was in high school it was called home ec. My mother told me that in her day it was domestic science, which has a nice professional ring to it. But whatever it's called…I hated it. It was required in our freshman year. The only thing that saved me from failing it was having rheumatic fever that spring, thus getting an Incomplete instead of F. I was grateful until senior year, when I had to take the last semester again.

The sewing part was pure torture. Rank beginners got to hem dishtowels, but those of us who'd been in 4-H went straight to sewing a cotton dress. I should never have raised my hand when Miss Bitter (yes, that was her real name) asked which of us had been in 4-H. As far as I was concerned, 4-H had been just slightly more fun than home ec. At least we had a few parties, and went to Pacific Northwest Expo, which was a big deal at that time. As part of our club duties we were all supposed to start a journal at the beginning of the year, listing the projects and activities we planned. Then we were to keep it updated as the year progressed. I wrote my entire journal the night before it was supposed to be turned in. Unfortunately, I wrote those beginning entries in the past tense, so my misdeed was glaringly obvious.

The cotton dress was a disaster. I snuck it home and spent many evenings ripping out mistakes while listening to "Your Hit Parade" on the radio. I snarled to a background of Eddie Fisher singing "Oh, My Papa" and Patti Page's "Doggie in the Window." After first sewing them in backwards, I finally conquered the sleeves. Completion deadline was looming when Mom took pity on me and finished it. She got a "D" for sewing the yoke wrong. Mom loved sewing just as much as I did, evidently.

Then the cooking semester began. Poor Miss Bitter had started the year pretty calmly, but she unraveled as time went on. We were too busy talking about boys and making whispered fun of her hairdo to pay attention. It looked like it had been styled by sticking her finger in an electrical outlet until her hair frizzed straight out from her head. By the time March rolled around, Miss Bitter was having trouble remembering what day it was, and what we were supposed to cook that day. She stored meat in the oven instead of the refrigerator, and since we didn't bake for many days, it was brown and vile-smelling by the time it was discovered. She sent girls down to the grocery store to buy supplies she'd forgotten to get the previous day, and their trip took long enough that only about 10 minutes of class was left when they got back. You can't cook much in 10 minutes.

I cheerfully put home ec out of my mind until senior year, when I had to repeat that last semester in order to graduate. Miss Bitter was gone by then, poor thing, and we had a young, energetic teacher. Since I was three years older than all the other girls in the class, I seemed very mature. Soon I was her informal assistant.

Evidently there were no state standards for the class at that time, because our cooking was definitely off the beaten path. "You're all going to have to fix boring and cheap things at home, or when you get married, so we're just going to have fun cooking," the teacher said. We learned how to make fudge, fancy cookies, quiche and elaborate salads. It was definitely fun, although I could have used training in the boring stuff. I'd once made cornbread which Dad said was the best he'd ever tasted, and Mom never let me near the stove again. It was her turf, and I'd better not try planting my flag on it. I could peel potatoes or scrub beets, but the oven was definitely off limits.

I did learn a few things in the class: how to make oil and vinegar salad dressing; how to cook fresh vegetables without boiling them to death, and especially, how to present a pretty plate. I'd never heard of varying the colors of food at a meal. Mom just had to cook whatever was available, and if it was all the same color…tough.

I got an "A" in home ec that time around, while still not able to cook or sew. Later, my poor husband was the guinea pig while I learned basic things like steak is to be broiled, not boiled, and you're never to put pasta in the pot before the water is boiling.

After the children came along, I taught myself to read patterns and sew. There were some weird products at first, but I improved.

Now I love to cook and sew. Go figure! Maybe home ec wasn't so bad after all! Miss Bitter would be pleased.

June, 2011

THE BLESSING OF TIME

When I look back on raising my kids, I like to think I did a reasonably good job…or at least that I tried my best. I can remember some golden highlights, and of course some black marks: times when I was short-tempered under stress, afternoons they spent in their darkened bedrooms not because they needed naps, but because I needed some "me time." (In my defense, they always fell asleep within 15 minutes, so they really did need naps.) But the thing I regret most of all is the time I didn't spend with them.

Back in my child-rearing era, the physical part of parenting was very important: seeing that they were fed, clothed, took their vitamins, had checkups, regular baths, shampoos, the right balance of toys – some fun and some educational – and fresh air and exercise. But I don't remember playing with them enough.

Oh, it happened a few times. Digging rivers and building roads in the dirt pile for Matchbox cars. The occasional tea-party. But there wasn't much in-depth quality time.

I was reminded of this lack the last time two-and-a-half year old grandson Jasper visited. He hurried in the front door, calling excitedly, "Where's the Play-Doh?" It had been new at his previous visit and he'd evidently been thinking about it all month. Soon we were at the kitchen table, elbow deep in Play-Doh. His current interest craze is Mighty Machine DVDs from the library, specifically about sawmills, so I rolled out logs and he cut them into lengths with his combination table-knife/crosscut saw. Then he searched through the toy box to find a truck worthy of hauling logs, and hauled them to the other end of the table. When we ran out of Play-Doh we smushed up the logs and started over again.

Why didn't I do this with my kids? I thought. I remember Play-Doh, how quickly the fresh, vibrant colors got mixed together and became uniformly blah, how little dried-up pieces turned up in strange places for days. But I don't remember sitting at the table with the kids, having fun without warning them not to mix the colors.

When Jasper arrives, I always ask him what he wants for dinner and he always requests meatballs. I mix the hamburger, rice and seasonings to make porcupine meatballs, we scrub our hands thoroughly and begin molding them. "Meatball one," I say, tossing mine into the casserole dish. Jasper echoes me. Somewhere around meatball three the tempo picks up. "Plopball three!" Jasper giggles, bouncing his into the dish. "Flopball four!" I respond. Soon we're slinging slopballs and squishballs and oopsballs faster and faster and Jasper is laughing so hard he can barely get the latest name out. I know I'll be reshaping meatballs as soon as I get him interested in something else, but it's great fun. I ask myself why I never did this with my own kids.

Then I remember. If dinner prep took too long, then dinner, baths and bedtime was late. My schedule was hopelessly broken, and there was still a load of laundry to fold.

Jasper's parents made the decision to put his security and happiness ahead of material possessions, and to live on only one salary for at least the first few years of his life. Our son Shawn worked while Becky completed her doctorate, gave birth and nursed Jasper. Then when he was almost two, she put her degree to work and Shawn became daytime caregiver. He is fully engaged with Jasper all day long: teaching, pretending, going to parks, museums, the zoo, the aquarium. Children's DVDs are a limited privilege, not a built-in babysitter. Jasper gets lots of exercise, outside when possible. If the weather is too rainy, they work out indoors. On our last visit Jasper demonstrated his ability to (almost) do a headstand. "Just try it, Grandma," he encouraged me. I told him no, I couldn't do a headstand. "Yes, you can! Just practice, practice, practice!" was his advice.

When Mommy's home, Jasper has her complete attention and love. They talk about all the things he did that day. They cook together, not worrying about a trashed kitchen or a late meal. They go to Whole Foods, and take neighborhood walks. Every evening he picks out the three library books for her to read to him at bedtime.

As a family, they attend free local festivities and multicultural events, of which Seattle has many, and outings with friends who also have children.

I'm sure that now and then Daddy gets a little stir-crazy, and I know Mommy often misses her little boy, but it works for them. The result is a child who is bright, creative, generous, and by turns rowdy or sensitive. He gives love freely because he is freely loved.

Will Jasper remember this special time when he's grown? I think so.

I'm sure my kids don't remember nutritional meals and neatly-folded clean clothes. I hope they remember long story sessions and the rare Matchbook car playground and tea-party. I wish there had been more.

June, 2011

I NEVER DID LIKE SCRUBBING TOILETS

I gave myself a treat the other day - two hours of Merry Maids time.

It was wonderful, although my tough-scrubbing mother was probably spinning in her grave at the thought of her daughter hiring someone to do her housework. Mom would have said that having a housekeeper or a cleaning lady meant you were getting "uppity". So this was a new experience for me.

My socio-economic level must be the folks who think it's perfectly fine to hire anything done that's too complex to do yourself, like computer programming, television repair or electrical wiring. But we scrub our own toilets. However, when I learned that was included in the price I was quoted, I quickly decided that the sound of stiff bristles on porcelain was music to my ears, as long as somebody else was propelling the brush. And when they said that cleaning the surfaces of the refrigerator and kitchen stove was also included, I just tuned out that little whisper of conscience that said I was being lazy. All I'd asked for in the kitchen was cleaning the woodwork and cupboards, but hey…maybe these girls would get in trouble if they didn't do the whole nine yards.

What a blissful morning that was! I worked on a computer project while the aroma of bleach and cleaning products wafted through the house. The sound of someone cheerfully whistling while they scoured the tub surround seemed like a symphony.

Admiring my sparkling kitchen, I understood how the kids used to look at a newly-tidied toy-room and immediately want to haul out all the Fisher-Price stuff and make a brightly-colored town that covered the entire floor and spilled out into the hallway. I felt just like that. I was inspired to do something Betty Crocker-ish or Martha Steward-ish, like alphabetizing the contents of the spice rack, and emptying original packages into clear glass jars, so that beans, rice and pasta became counter décor. I managed to limit the creative urge to buying new shelf paper.

Then I attacked the contents of the kitchen and dining room table, where I'd piled everything from the cupboards. I got out a black trash bag and ruthlessly weeded out anything past its pull-date, and the mystery items that I couldn't even remember buying, much less what I thought I was going to do with them. The top shelf items that I can only reach on a step-stool were the first to go.

Did I really think I was going to make fruitcake with this container of candied fruits that was now clumped into a multicolored mass frosted white with sugar? And just what is citron, anyhow?

Kool-Aid? Good grief, I haven't stirred up a pitcher of the red or green stuff since the two older grandkids outgrew their taste for it. They're now 29 and 24. I suppose I could keep it for little grandson Jasper, but today we know the effects of too much sugar and Red Dye #10. Into the trash bag.

Hmm. Dried prunes. Must have bought those for snacks on a trip, which was an unreasonable expectation. Nobody ate them. Everybody knows the best car snacks are cashews and cheese doodles. Wait. Maybe I could look up the recipe for the prune cake Mom used to make. It was delicious. No, I'd have to chop all those prunes into tiny bits. Besides, I haven't made a cake from scratch in so long I can't even remember when.

Lentils left from the time I was going to try Middle Eastern cooking. It was a one-time-only kind of event. Our taste-buds are more Midwest USA than Mideast Asian. Into the trash bag. No, save them. Like beans, dry lentils last forever. When a big disaster strikes and people are starving, we'll still have our lentils and beans.

Hmm, packages of spaghetti sauce mix. I've used Ragu in a jar forever, so these must be antique. Yes, here's the date: Use by 07-10-2001. How embarrassing!

On to the drawer of when-would-I-ever-use-this stuff. A package of candy eyes that must have been intended for gingerbread men. Let's see, how many years ago was it that I gave up trying to make gingerbread men, or any other rolled cookies? Quite a few. I can remember grandkids rummaging through the drawer trying to find enough matching candles to trim a cake, and asking, "Hey, Grandma, what are these funny black and white eyes for?" Which brings us to the remnants of many, many boxes of birthday candles, with never more than four or five of matching size, style or color. Quite a few have softened to strange shapes. Well, you know the old saying, "If you can't stand the heat, get out of the kitchen." It applies to birthday candles, too. Into the trash bag.

Finished at last. My Betty Crocker thirst has been slaked, and I have two empty kitchen shelves to fill with more impulse items. Thank you, Merry Maids! I'm off to the supermarket.

July, 2011

THE REVISED ERRAND LIST

I had my errand list and keys in hand, headed for the car. Then I remembered the errand lists of the good old days when I was a working mom, before the kids flew the nest. I got tired just thinking about it, and had to go back inside for an invigorating cup of peppermint tea. Besides, there was no rush.

Oh, I was organized in my Betty Crocker days. I posted the coming week's menus on Sunday, based on what the grocery store meat and produce specials had been when I shopped the day before. Careful planning went into the task. Bacon and egg breakfasts alternated with cold cereal or oatmeal, never the same thing every morning. The printed school lunch menu was consulted for which days the kids would buy, and which evenings I'd pack sandwiches, carrot sticks, cookies and fruit for the next day. Simple dinners or crockpot dishes were scheduled for evenings with a lot of after-school activities, and on the nights we were all home the dinners were nicer…balanced and, hopefully, tasty and appealing. (This despite the son who sullenly demanded, "Why don't we ever have anything good, like Spaghettios?")

Back then, all the errands had to be run on the weekend. Oh, there were a few things close to the office that I could handle during lunch time: drop off cleaning, stop at the bank. Some could be done after work if I left a few minutes early: drop off a kid for tightening braces or a piano lesson. But most waited until Saturday. The list was usually something like this:

- Hit the two yard sales that advertised canning jars.
- Drop off casserole dish for friend with new baby.
- Pick up my portable typewriter, repaired and supposedly good as new. The grandparents will be glad to start getting letters again.
- Garden shop – tomato, pepper, cucumber plants. (Note to self: It's finally do-or-die year for garden. No success this year, no garden next year.)

- Farm produce stand – asparagus and peppers. Russ loves pickled asparagus, even if it is a giant pain to preserve.
- Drop sewing machine off for repair. Plead and grovel for a quick job. (Note to self – never again try to mend a tent on a home sewing machine.)
- Fabric store – jeans patches, elastic, seersucker for pajamas.
- Cake decoration shop – new frosting tips and colors for bake sale cupcakes promised PTA.
- Grocery store – fill back of station wagon, knowing it'll be gone by next Thursday.
- Pick up kids, go to library. Help the two younger ones pick out storybooks, make sure the older two don't get "Lolita" or "Deliverance" or "Peyton Place". Steal 20 minutes for myself, if possible.

Whew, home at last! And they wondered why I was grouchy, and dinner was spaghettios! On the up-side, that made one kid happy.

In comparison, here's what today's quiet Friday list looks like:

- Hit the yard sale that advertised TOYS! TOYS! TOYS! (Still trying to fill the yard and toy-room for young grandson Jasper, years after selling all our toys at yard sales.)
- Pick up a Costco roast chicken for friend who had hip surgery. Not as much fun as bringing home a new baby, and takes much longer to recuperate. And roast chicken's not as good as my specialty casserole, but SO much easier.
- Garden shop – look for container plants that tolerate sun, neglect, and don't have to be weeded or dead-headed.
- Gourmet food shop – buy some pickled asparagus for Russ.
- Sewing center – get manual for new sewing machine, to replace the booklet I lost. I'm going to learn to make button-holes on that thing if it kills me!
- Fabric store – browse through in leisurely fashion to see if there's anything I absolutely can't resist, even if I don't know what I'll sew out of it.

- Jennie Mae's – check for new gluten-, dairy- and ovo-free treats for grandson. Don't forget pizza crust and muffin mix.
- Grocery store – strawberries (no more U-pick for us, thank you), lots of the items we couldn't afford when feeding a nest of six but can enjoy now that the fledglings have flown. Oh, yes, rice cheese to go on Jasper's safe pizza. And coconut yogurt and ice cream for his next visit.
- Encore Books – Buy that out-of-print special order he found me, cheaper than internet; also some of my guilty pleasure mysteries and science fiction.
- Library – pick up my on-line requests, chosen from book club reviews. Seldom buy anything from Literary Guild, but their book reviews come in handy.

Ah, home again. I feel like I've frittered the day away browsing for fun stuff. But come to think of it, I'm a little tired…too tired to cook dinner. Seafood sounds good, or maybe Italian. But first I'll have a glass of iced peppermint tea and relax while I think about the benefits of the empty nest. We might have a late dinner!

July, 2011

NATURE CALLS, BUT HE DOESN'T LISTEN

Our younger daughter recently told us a funny potty-training story. Seems she and two of her co-teachers were working on a school project at home, so the other two could bring along their young sons. Mom of the littlest boy mentioned she was worried about whether Jack, about two-and-a-half, was ready for potty training.

When the two boys brought their juice boxes and toys under the table where the women worked, mom got her answer as she heard Jack ask, "So, Braden, know much about diaper stuff?"

"I dunno," the older toddler replied. "Why?"

"Well, mine really needs changed," Jack said hopefully.

With a firmed-up mother, Jack soon proved remarkably ready.

I thought our oldest, Luanne, was ready when we started the project with her. In the warm summer weather she could play in training panties and tee-shirt, making the job easy. Then we began running out of training panties. Turns out she was getting dry ones out of the drawer, and with her sandbox shovel was giving the wet ones shallow burials under the rosebushes.

Our younger two kids never seemed ready. I worried that their huge night diapers made of old receiving blankets would make them bow-legged. Then the children finally got the message. "I have to go potty" joined requests for water and milk to postpone sleep. I wondered which was most harmful to a child: being bow-legged, or the memory of their slitted-eyed mother's foot tapping ominously near the potty, while their angelic smiles tried to atone for the lack of urine tinkling against plastic.

Our grandson Jasper seems very ready. In fact, he was potty-trained for two beautiful days. He even gave his folks enough warning that they got him to a bathroom at Target in time. Then on the third morning he refused the underpants. That wasn't so surprising. He'd much rather be naked, letting all four of his cheeks be cooled by Mother Nature as he plays. But he agreed to a diaper.

I can picture the wheels turning in that curly little head. "They're enjoying this far too much," Jasper tells Jasper. "All that squealing and clapping and telling me what a big boy I am, and giving me a star to stick on that stupid chart over my potty. Do they deserve that much fun? No, they do not. Yesterday's trip to the park was far shorter than usual. And the after-nap snack was definitely inferior. Gluten-free pretzels, chicken chunks and apple juice. Same old, same old. Well, no more Mr. Nice Guy. They want to see somebody jump through hoops, let them get a puppy. Or a monkey. Yeah, a monkey…that'd be fun!"

He just doesn't want his play time interrupted by trips to the bathroom. Or by diaper changes, either. Seeing him squatted by his Tonka truck, red-faced and intent, you'll ask him if he needs to go potty and he'll bark, "No!" Afterward, even if plants droop over limply when he walks by, he'll swear he doesn't need a fresh diaper.

I think shrewd bargaining is the only answer here. The bargaining chip has to be something important, though. You make an offer. If Jasper goes in the potty all day, at bedtime he can watch a new DVD, "Fisher-Price Little People Discover Things That Go". No potty, no DVD. Jasper agrees. Bedtime is far away. Who knows what will happen by then. A few hugs, kisses and angelic smiles will sway the parental unit, anyhow.

Now comes the prep time. Warn the nearest neighbors what's coming, so they won't call Child Protective Services. In fact, they might want to spend the evening with friends elsewhere. Put the new DVD and the remote in some safe place, like the top of the refrigerator. Get Jasper fresh shorts and clean up the little puddles he leaves behind when he ignores nature's call.

Harden your hearts for bedtime, so those tight hugs and butterfly kisses don't do you in. Endure a huge tantrum, followed by a sobbed litany of "I want the movie! I want the movie!" Stand by Jasper's bed after he finally cries himself to sleep, face red, nose runny, long lashes clumped together with tears, chest still shuddering with the echo of sobs.

Stay firm next morning, when Jasper's first words won't be "Can I have bananas on my oatmeal?" They'll be, "I want to watch the "Little People Discover Things That Go" movie!" Re-run day one. Ask the neighbors if they're planning anything out-of-town for the weekend.

Probably on day three he'll plop himself down on the potty-chair. Or maybe day four.

One request. Don't plan this for Grandma and Grandpa's house. We all know Grandma would be first one to get the step-stool to reach the refrigerator top.

Better yet, maybe when Jasper starts pre-school he'll have a friend who "knows about diaper stuff".

August, 2011

REST IN PEACE, OLD FRIEND

Ever since our daughter Katy's loveable dog, Ben, started to get old, I've hoped that the Grim Reaper would call for me before Ben. I knew how painful it would be for Katy and therefore for me…knowing her grief, and missing the furry little granddog myself. Being a natural coward, I'd rather have skipped that pain. But Ben won…or lost, as the case may be. Cancer took him this August.

I think pets should have roughly the same life expectancy as humans. That way, we'd only know that loss once or twice in our lifetime, instead of over and over again. I'm not talking about pets like gerbils, parakeets or goldfish, but cats and dogs. Especially dogs. Their DNA is nothing like ours, but some of their traits are very human. Their love, loyalty, protectiveness, and the desire and ability to give comfort probably weren't parts of their personality when they first skulked around the caveman's campfire to snatch scraps of meat, but over all those years, the traits developed.

Ben was a cocker spaniel/American Eskimo mix, a soft, white, furry ball of fun even as he aged. After 12 years with Katy, he still loved to play right up until the worst part of his illness. When we visited, he'd bounce out to greet us, tongue lolling in a doggy grin, chin down on his front paws and rear up in the air, tail wagging furiously.

Katy and Ben accompanied us on many trips, so we got acquainted with pet-friendly motels of the northwest. It was a lot like traveling with the kids again…stopping often for bathroom breaks, cold drinks and a chance to run off steam. The main difference was the lack of fighting over who got to the window seat when we got back in the car.

He was always eager for the next adventure. We have pictures of the last time Russ and our two daughters hiked the Klickitat Trail. At the beginning Ben is shown jauntily trotting along. The picture taken near the end shows him being carried by Katy. Exhaustion and thorns took the fun out of the hike.

Among Ben's many strange fears was uncarpeted floors; the only thing that could lure him onto the tiled kitchen floor was the prospect of a treat. And did he love those treats! We all learned to save the last bite of whatever we were eating for Ben. He had a way of placing his paw on your knee and looking up at you with those pleading, cocker spaniel eyes, sort of like Oliver Twist holding out his empty bowl and saying, "Please, sir, I want more." It earned him the last bite every time. I always made him dog cookies for Christmas, with bacon grease instead of oil, and powdered beef bouillon for flavor. He loved them, and knew he'd get one as a reward after distasteful things like nail clipping or ear cleaning.

Ben couldn't talk, but he definitely understood some words. "Cookie" was one, and "go in the car", "grandma and grandpa", "squirrel" and "bedtime".

"Bedtime" meant it was time to follow Katy down the hall and curl up by her bed. When I visited, he trotted into my bedroom and slept by my bed as soon as she went to school.

"Squirrel" was the word that caused him to rush to the window and bark frantically at the tree. He got the same eager look when he heard "kitty", so we didn't say that very often.

He was a needy little dog, always following close behind Katy. If she wasn't around, he settled for me. I never thought there'd be room for a dog to curl up in my cramped computer work station, but he proved there was.

Ben's health started to fail last Christmas. After a surgery he had to wear a tee-shirt to protect his incision. With his front legs in the sleeves he looked embarrassed as he pawed open his Christmas cookies, but he managed.

He continued to deteriorate, and around Easter the vet said it was cancer, and he might live another year, but probably not. Katy vowed that as long as he was getting any enjoyment out of life, he would live. Up until a month before his death, he sometimes played, and always begged for the last bite, even when he was having chemo.

In August the time came when he threw up everything he ate; then didn't eat at all. He was too weak to follow Katy from room to room as he'd always done, and had spells of tremors and irregular breathing. It was cruel to let someone you loved suffer so.

The vet gave Katy an impression of Ben's paw-print in a plaque, and he was gone. Rest in peace, Ben. You were a good friend, and we'll always remember you.

If I make it to Heaven, there'd better be a little white dog bouncing up to meet his grandma, or I'm not staying!

September, 2011

GOLDEN SEPTEMBER

I wonder why autumn always make me feel so nostalgic. I used to think maybe it was caused by the scent of burning leaves, but that can't be it. Now you cram them into big bags for pickup, because it's not legal to burn them. Nevertheless, nostalgia somehow sneaks in.

When the mornings get crispy while the days stay soft and warm, my mind drifts back to my childhood. The Septembers I remember were golden…not a raindrop in sight. I know that couldn't possibly have been true in the Portland-Vancouver area, but that's how I remember it. In my memory I walk home from school in the warm afternoon, glad to be out of the stuffy classroom. I scuff dust all over my new shoes, the ones that feel like an instrument of torture after going barefoot all summer. While sauntering along I'm praying for an earthquake to cancel school before my mother finds out I can't learn long division. Not a big enough earthquake to kill people, just stop classes. Maybe it could be right under the school building. During the night, of course, so nobody gets hurt.

I cut through the orchard, inspecting the filbert trees and wishing you could eat them right off the tree, like apples, instead of waiting for them to dry enough for the husks to slip off. I settle for a Gravenstein apple, a perfect combination of sweet and tart. Or maybe I'll detour through the garden and pluck a tomato, ripe, sun-warmed and bursting with flavor. Oh, heck! They're better with salt, and if I go inside for the saltshaker, I'll get drafted for some chore I'd prefer to miss. Maybe I'll just pull some carrots. I can wash them with the garden hose and Mom won't know I'm home for awhile yet.

Eventually I have to go inside and change into play-clothes, which always seems like false advertising to me, because I won't be playing. This time of year Mom is up to her elbows in canning, and that means helping.

Mom asks how was school, and I tell her good. She asks how I did in arithmetic, and I tell her fine, completely skipping over long division. Then it's time for kitchen duty.

I don't mind snapping green beans. Scrubbing cucumbers and snipping dill sprigs for pickles isn't too bad. Slipping the skins off peaches and beets after Mom has blanched them is actually kind of fun. But when it comes to peeling pears or grating cabbage for sauerkraut, the fun stops. On the plus side, the kitchen smells like Mom is making grape jelly. If she is, there'll be a saucer of what Dad calls "calf slobber" and refuses to eat…the foam skimmed off the top of the kettle. With homemade bread and butter, it's delicious.

If there's no canning going on, I'll still be busy on a golden September late afternoon. I'll be given a basket and instructions: "Take the pitchfork and dig up the biggest potato plant. Knock off all the dirt from the spuds and wash them in the hose; no sense bringing half the garden inside. And pick eight ears of corn, nice fat, heavy ones. Oh, and some tomatoes and a couple of cucumbers. That should take care of supper."

Maybe I'll be sent to gather the eggs. I always throw a handful of chicken feed to the far side of their pen. When they swoop out to eat it, I race inside the now-empty chicken house and slam down the little door leading to their pen. I know I'm too old to be afraid of chickens, but that rooster seems to think his mission in life is to rush at any intruder, flapping his wings fiercely and swearing in rooster language. Even the hens get crabby if you have to reach under them to get the egg they think they're going to hatch.

I might have to churn…sit out on the porch with the square glass Dazey churn between my knees and turn that handle until it feels like my arm might fall off. When the weather's warm it takes forever for the butter to come.

I've been smart enough to fail at learning to milk the cow, but I get stuck with roundup duty when she decides not to come to the barn as twilight approaches. I hurry down the lane and warily enter the woods, thinking about bears and panthers. They're never on my mind when we play here in the daytime, but it's different when the light starts to fade. If I'm lucky the cow will be in a clear little meadow area; if not I have to scramble through bushes and scrub to find her, which proves to me all over again just how stupid cows are. I breathe a sigh of relief when she's sauntering ahead of me up the lane. Safe one more time!

Dad gets home from work. The golden day is dimming as we gather around the supper table. Life is good. I'll worry about long division tomorrow.

Made in the USA
San Bernardino, CA
05 April 2016